Algebra 2

Student Practice Workbook

+ Two Full-Length Algebra 2 Exams

Math Notion

www.MathNotion.com

Algebra 2

Algebra 2

Algebra 2

Published in the United State of America By

The Math Notion

Web: WWW.MathNotion.com

Email: info@Mathnotion.com

Copyright © 2021 by the Math Notion. All rights reserved. No part of this publication may be reproduced, stored in a retrieval system, or transmitted in any form or by any means, electronic, mechanical, photocopying, recording, scanning, or otherwise, except as permitted under Section 107 or 108 of the 1976 United States Copyright Ac, without permission of the author.

All inquiries should be addressed to the Math Notion.

ISBN: 978-1-63620-100-9

> Algebra 2

The Math Notion

Michael Smith has been a math instructor for over a decade now. He launched the Math Notion. Since 2006, we have devoted our time to both teaching and developing exceptional math learning materials. As a test prep company, we have worked with thousands of students. We have used the feedback of our students to develop a unique study program that can be used by students to drastically improve their math scores fast and effectively. We have more than a thousand Math learning books including:

- **SAT Math Prep**
- **ACT Math Prep**
- **Algebra 1 & 2 Workbook**
- **CLEP College Algebra Workbook**
- **CLEP College Mathematics Workbook**
- –many **Math Education Workbooks, Study Guides, Practice and Exercise Books**

As an experienced Math test preparation company, we have helped many students raise their standardized test scores—and attend the colleges of their dreams: We tutor online and in person, we teach students in large groups, and we provide training materials and textbooks through our website and through Amazon.

You can contact us via email at:

info@MathNotion.com

Algebra 2

Get the Targeted Practice You Need to Ace the Algebra 2 Exam!

Algebra 2 Book includes easy-to-follow instructions, helpful examples, and plenty of algebraic practice problems to assist students to master each concept, brush up their problem-solving skills, and create confidence.

The Algebra 2 practice book provides numerous opportunities to evaluate basic skills along with abundant remediation and intervention activities. It is a skill that permits you to quickly master intricate information and produce better leads in less time.

Students can boost their test-taking skills by taking the book's two practice algebra tests. All test questions answered and explained in detail.

Important Features of the Algebra 2 Book:

- A **complete review** of Algebra 2 exam topics,
- Over 2,500 practice problems covering all topics tested,
- The most important concepts you need to know,
- Clear and concise, easy-to-follow sections,
- Well designed for enhanced learning and interest,
- Hands-on experience with all question types,
- **2 full-length practice tests** with detailed answer explanations,
- Cost-Effective Pricing,

Powerful algebra exercises to help you avoid traps and pacing yourself to beat the algebra 2 exam. Students will gain valuable experience and raise their confidence by taking algebra 2 practice tests, learning about test structure, and gaining a deeper understanding of what is tested on the algebra. If ever there was a book to respond to the pressure to increase students' exam scores, this is it.

Algebra 2

WWW.MathNotion.COM

… So Much More Online!

✓ FREE Math Lessons

✓ More Math Learning Books!

✓ Mathematics Worksheets

✓ Online Math Tutors

For a PDF Version of This Book

Please Visit WWW.MathNotion.com

Algebra 2

Contents

Chapter 1 : Review of The Linear Functions 11
   Finding Slope 12
   Graphing Linear Equations 13
   Graphing Linear Inequalities 14
   Writing Linear Equations 15
   Graphing Horizontal and Vertical Lines 17
   Rate of change 18
   x and y intercepts 18
   Slope–intercept Form 19
   Point–slope Form 20
   Equation of Parallel or Perpendicular Lines 21
   Graphing Absolute Value Equations 22
   Answers of Worksheets 23

Chapter 2 : System of Equations 28
   Solving Systems of Equations by Substitution 29
   Solving Systems of Equations by Elimination 30
   Systems of Equations Word Problems 31
   Three Variables System of Equations 32
   Answers of Worksheets 33

Chapter 3 : Radicals Expressions 34
   Simplifying Radical Expressions 35
   Adding and Subtracting Radical Expressions 36
   Multiplying Radical Expressions 37
   Simplifying Radical Expressions Involving Fractions 38
   Answers of Worksheets 39

Chapter 4 : Functions Operations and Quadratic 41
   Relations and Functions 42
   Evaluating Function 43
   Adding and Subtracting Functions 44
   Multiplying and Dividing Functions 45
   Composition of Functions 46

Algebra 2

Quadratic Equation	47
Solving Quadratic Equations	48
Quadratic Formula and the Discriminant	49
Graphing Quadratic Functions	50
Quadratic Inequalities	51
Domain and Range of Radical Functions	52
Solving Radical Equations	53
Answers of Worksheets	54
Chapter 5 : Monomials and Polynomials	**59**
GCF of Monomials	60
Factoring Quadratics	61
Factoring by Grouping	62
GCF and Powers of Monomials	63
Writing Polynomials in Standard Form	64
Simplifying Polynomials	65
Adding and Subtracting Polynomials	66
Multiplying Monomials	67
Multiplying and Dividing Monomials	68
Multiplying a Polynomial and a Monomial	69
Multiplying Binomials	70
Factoring Trinomials	71
Operations with Polynomials	72
Answers of Worksheets	73
Chapter 6 : Complex Numbers	**79**
Adding and Subtracting Complex Numbers	80
Multiplying and Dividing Complex Numbers	81
Graphing Complex Numbers	82
Rationalizing Imaginary Denominators	83
Answers of Worksheets	84
Chapter 7 : Sequences and Series	**85**
Arithmetic Sequences	86
Geometric Sequences	87
Comparing Arithmetic and Geometric Sequences	88
Finite Geometric Series	89
Infinite Geometric Series	90
Answers of Worksheets	91

Algebra 2

Chapter 8 : Rational Expressions...94
   Simplifying and Graphing Rational Expressions 95
   Adding and Subtracting Rational Expressions 96
   Multiplying and Dividing Rational Expressions 97
   Solving Rational Equations and Complex Fractions 98
   Answers of Worksheets 99

Chapter 9 : Matrices...101
   Adding and Subtracting Matrices..102
   Matrix Multiplication 103
   Finding Determinants of a Matrix 104
   Finding Inverse of a Matrix 105
   Matrix Equations 106
   Answers of Worksheets 107

Chapter 10 : Logarithms...109
   Rewriting Logarithms..110
   Evaluating Logarithms...111
   Properties of Logarithms..112
   Natural Logarithms...113
   Exponential Equations and Logarithms 114
   Solving Logarithmic Equations 115
   Answers of Worksheets 116

Chapter 11 : Conic Sections 119
   Equation of a Parabola 120
   Focus, Vertex, and Directrix of a Parabola 121
   Standard Form of a Circle..122
   Equation of Each Ellipse..123
   Hyperbola in Standard Form 124
   Conic Sections in Standard Form 125
   Answers of Worksheets 126

Chapter 12 : Trigonometric Functions 129
   Trig ratios of General Angles 130
   Sketch Each Angle in Standard Position 131
   Finding Co-terminal Angles and Reference Angles 132
   Angles and Angle Measure..133
   Evaluating Trigonometric Functions 134
   Missing Sides and Angles of a Right Triangle 135

Algebra 2

    Arc Length and Sector Area 136

    Answers of Worksheets 137

Chapter 13 : Statistics and Probability **139**

    Probability Problems 140

    Factorials 141

    Combinations and Permutations 142

    Answers of Worksheets 143

Chapter 14 : Algebra 2 Practice Tests **145**

    Algebra 2 Practice Test 1 149

    Algebra 2 Practice Test 2 157

Chapter 15 : Answers and Explanations **165**

    Answer Key 165

    Practice Tests 1 167

    Practice Tests 2 173

Algebra 2

Chapter 1:
Review of The Linear Functions

Topics that you'll practice in this chapter:

- ✓ Finding Slope,
- ✓ Graphing Linear Equations,
- ✓ Graphing Linear Inequalities,
- ✓ Writing Linear Equations,
- ✓ Graphing Horizontal and Vertical lines
- ✓ Finding Rate of Change,
- ✓ Find the x–intercept and y–intercept,
- ✓ Slope-Intercept Form Equations,
- ✓ Point-Slope Form Equations,
- ✓ Equation of parallel or perpendicular lines,
- ✓ Graphing Lines of Equations,
- ✓ Graphing Absolute Value Equations

"Life is a math equation. In order to gain the most, you have to know how to convert negatives into positives." – Anonymous

Algebra 2

Finding Slope

✎ **Find the slope of each line.**

1) $y = x + 8$

2) $y = -3x + 5$

3) $y = 2x + 12$

4) $y = -4x + 19$

5) $y = 11 + 6x$

6) $y = 7 - 5x$

7) $y = 8x + 19$

8) $y = -9x + 20$

9) $y = -7x + 4$

10) $y = 3x - 8$

11) $y = \frac{1}{3}x + 8$

12) $y = -\frac{4}{5}x + 9$

13) $-3x + 6y = 30$

14) $4x + 4y = 16$

15) $3y - x = 10$

16) $8y - x = 5$

✎ **Find the slope of the line through each pair of points.**

17) $(2, 3), (7, 10)$

18) $(-3, 5), (2, 15)$

19) $(5, -3), (1, 9)$

20) $(-5, -5), (10, 25)$

21) $(22, 3), (7, 18)$

22) $(-16, 8), (-7, 26)$

23) $(25, 11), (29, 19)$

24) $(26, -19), (14, 17)$

25) $(22, -13), (20, -11)$

26) $(19, 7), (15, -3)$

27) $(5, 7), (11, 19)$

28) $(52, -62), (40, 70)$

Algebra 2

Graphing Linear Equations

✎ **Sketch the graph of each line.**

1) $y = x - 2$ 2) $y = -3x + 2$ 3) $x + y = 0$

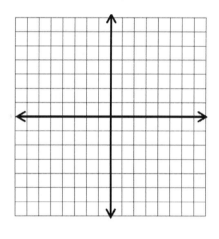 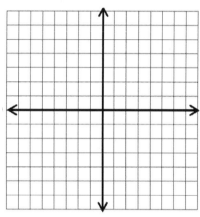 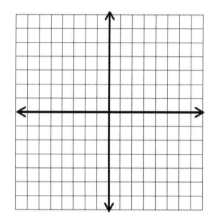

4) $x + y = -3$ 5) $2x + 3y = -4$ 6) $y - 3x + 6 = 0$

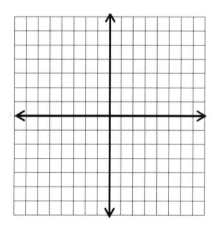 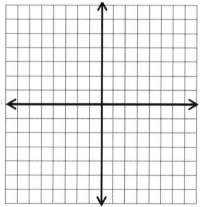 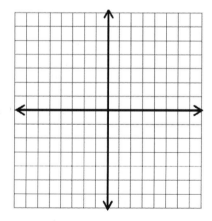

Algebra 2

Graphing Linear Inequalities

✎ **Sketch the graph of each linear inequality.**

1) $y > 4x - 5$

2) $y < 2x + 4$

3) $y \leq -5x - 2$

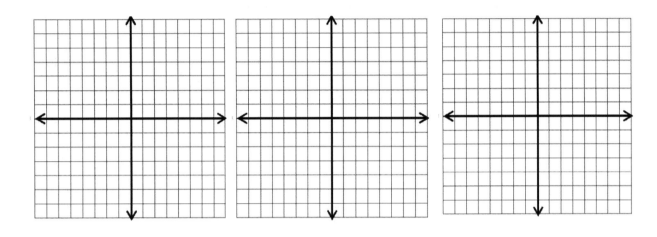

4) $4y \geq 12 + 4x$

5) $-12y < 3x - 24$

6) $5y \geq -15x + 10$

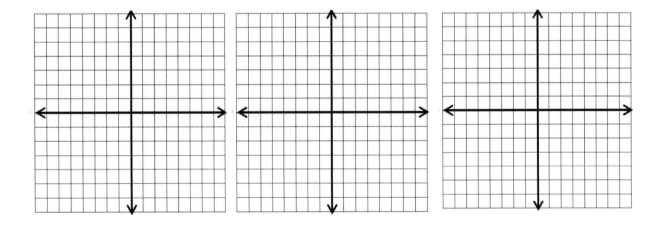

Algebra 2

Writing Linear Equations

✎ **Write the equation of the line through the given points.**

1) Through: $(2, -5), (3, 9)$

2) Through: $(-6, 3), (3, 12)$

3) Through: $(10, 7), (5, 27)$

4) Through: $(15, 11), (3, -1)$

5) Through: $(24, 17), (12, -7)$

6) Through: $(8, 29), (4, -7)$

7) Through: $(20, -16), (12, 0)$

8) Through: $(-3, 10), (2, -5)$

9) Through: $(-6, 17), (4, -3)$

10) Through: $(-8, 22), (5, -4)$

11) Through: $(9, 27), (3, -3)$

12) Through: $(11, 32), (9, 4)$

13) Through: $(-3, 13), (-4, 0)$

14) Through: $(-5, 5), (5, 15)$

15) Through: $(18, -32), (11, 3)$

16) Through: $(-4, 25), (4, -15)$

✎ **Find the answer for each problem.**

17) What is the equation of a line with slope 6 and intercept 12? _____

18) What is the equation of a line with slope -11 and intercept -4? _____

19) What is the equation of a line with slope -3 and passes through point $(5, 2)$? _____

20) What is the equation of a line with slope -5 and passes through point $(-2, -1)$? _____

21) The slope of a line is -10 and it passes through point $(-3, 0)$. What is the equation of the line? _____

22) The slope of a line is 8 and it passes through point $(0, 7)$. What is the equation of the line? _____

Algebra 2

✎ **Find the value of** b**: The line that passes through each pair of points has the given slope.**

1) $(5, -4), (2, b), m = 1$

2) $(b, -4), (-4, 1), m = -\frac{1}{3}$

3) $(-4, b), (4, 8), m = \frac{1}{2}$

4) $(0, 3), (b, 8), m = 1\frac{2}{3}$

✎ **Write the slope intercept form of the equation of each line.**

1)
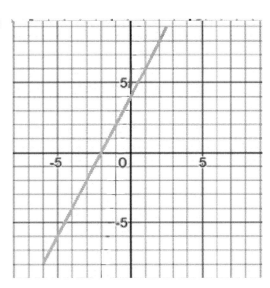

2)
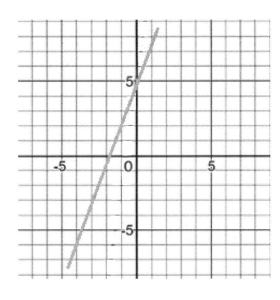

3)
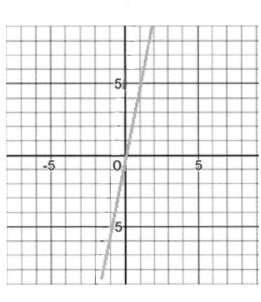

4)
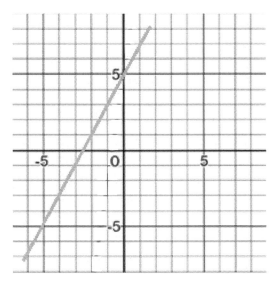

WWW.MathNotion.Com

Algebra 2

Graphing Horizontal and Vertical Lines

✎ **Sketch the graph of each line.**

1) $y = 3$

2) $y = -1$

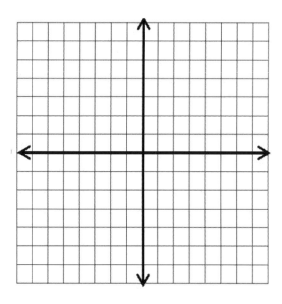 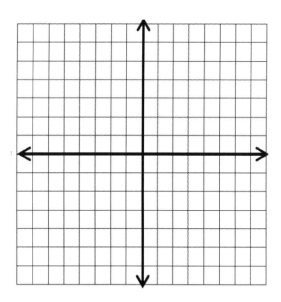

3) $x = 0$

4) $x = 3$

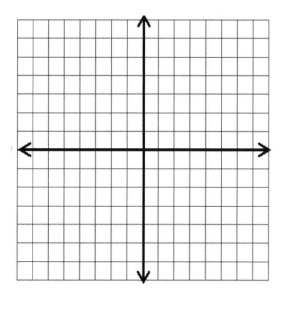 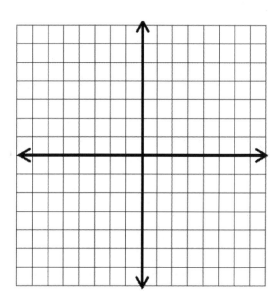

WWW.MathNotion.Com

Algebra 2

Rate of change

✎ **What is the average rate of change of the function?**

1) $f(x) = 3x^2 + 5$, from $x = 3$ to $x = 6$?

2) $f(x) = -2x^2 - 4$, from $x = 2$ to $x = 4$?

3) $f(x) = x^3 + 3$, from $x = 1$ to $x = 2$?

x and y intercepts

✎ **Find the x and y intercepts for the following equations.**

1) $5x + 3y = 15$

2) $y = x + 8$

3) $4x = y + 16$

4) $x + y = -2$

5) $4x - 3y = 7$

6) $7y - 5x + 10 = 0$

7) $\frac{3}{7}x + \frac{1}{4}y + \frac{2}{3} = 0$

8) $3x - 21 = 0$

9) $24 - 4y = 0$

10) $-2x - 6y + 42 = 12$

Algebra 2

Slope–intercept Form

✎ **Write the slope–intercept form of the equation of each line.**

1) $-14x + y = 6$

2) $-2(7x + y) = 24$

3) $-8x - 16y = -48$

4) $5x + 14 = -3y$

5) $x - 3y = 12$

6) $18x - 12y = -6$

7) $28x - 14y = -56$

8) $7x - 4y + 25 = 0$

9) $-\frac{1}{3}y = -2x + 3$

10) $5 - y - 4x = 0$

11) $-y = -6x - 9$

12) $10x + 5y = -15$

13) $3(x + y + 2) = 0$

14) $y - 4 = x + 3$

15) $3(y + 3) = 2(x - 3)$

16) $\frac{3}{4}y + \frac{1}{4}x + \frac{5}{4} = 0$

Algebra 2

Point–slope Form

✎ **Find the slope of the following lines. Name a point on each line.**

1) $y = 2(x + 3)$

2) $y + 4 = \dfrac{1}{3}(x - 1)$

3) $y + 3 = -1.5x$

4) $y - 3 = \dfrac{1}{2}(x - 2)$

5) $y + 2 = 0.4\,(x + 3)$

6) $y - 8 = -3x$

7) $y - 12 = -3\,(x - 8)$

8) $y + 14 = 0$

9) $y + 18 = 2\,(x + 5)$

10) $y - 17 = -8\,(x - 3)$

✎ **Write an equation in point–slope form for the line that passes through the given point with the slope provided.**

11) $(2, -3), m = 4$

12) $(-7, 4), m = \dfrac{1}{5}$

13) $(0, -6), m = -2$

14) $(-a, b), m = m$

15) $(-9, 1), m = 3$

16) $(3, 0), m = -5$

17) $(-4, 11), m = \dfrac{1}{3}$

18) $(0, 11), m = 0$

19) $\left(-\dfrac{1}{3}, 3\right), m = \dfrac{1}{5}$

20) $(0, 0), m = -3$

WWW.MathNotion.Com

Algebra 2

Equation of Parallel or Perpendicular Lines

✎ **Write an equation of the line that passes through the given point and is parallel to the given line.**

1) $(-1, -2), x + 3y = -11$

2) $(-4, 1), y = x - 5$

3) $(-2, 0), 2y = 5x - 3$

4) $(0, 0), -3y + 4x - 14 = 0$

5) $(1, 10), y + 15 = 0$

6) $(0, 7), -5x - y = -4$

7) $(-2, -1), y = \frac{4}{5}x + 3$

8) $(-2, 5), -8x + 5y = -18$

9) $(3, -2), y = -\frac{2}{5}x - 3$

10) $(-5, -5), 6x + 15y = -30$

✎ **Write an equation of the line that passes through the given point and is perpendicular to the given line.**

11) $(-2, -6), 3x + 4y = -8$

12) $(-\frac{1}{3}, \frac{3}{5}), 4x - 8y = -32$

13) $(2, -5), y = -5$

14) $(7, -2), x = 7$

15) $(0, -3), y = \frac{1}{2}x + 6$

16) $(\frac{3}{5}, \frac{2}{5}), y = -6x - 24$

17) $(-10, 0), y = \frac{5}{3}x - 15$

18) $(3, -5), y = x + 12$

19) $(-3, -1), y = \frac{7}{3}x - 4$

20) $(0, 0), y - 8x + 6 = 0$

WWW.MathNotion.Com

Algebra 2

Graphing Absolute Value Equations

✎ **Graph each equation.**

1) $y = |x + 4|$

2) $y = |x + 1|$

3) $y = -|x| - 1$

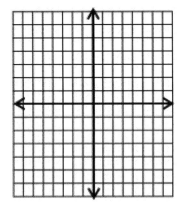 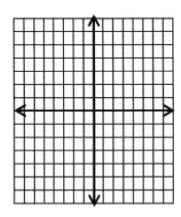 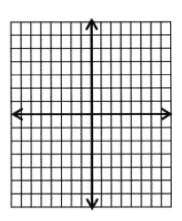

4) $y = |x - 2|$

5) $y = -|x - 2|$

6) $y = -2|2x + 2| + 4$

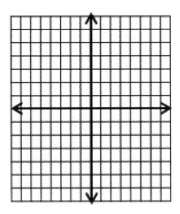 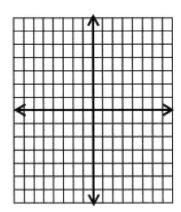 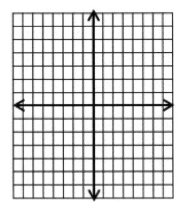

Algebra 2

Answers of Worksheets

Finding Slope

1) 1
2) −3
3) 2
4) −4
5) 6
6) −5
7) 8
8) −9
9) −7
10) 3
11) $\frac{1}{3}$
12) $-\frac{4}{5}$
13) $\frac{1}{2}$
14) −1
15) $\frac{1}{3}$
16) $\frac{1}{8}$
17) $\frac{7}{5}$
18) 2
19) −3
20) 2
21) −1
22) 2
23) 2
24) −3
25) −1
26) $\frac{5}{2}$
27) 2
28) −11

Graphing Linear Equations

1) $y = x - 2$

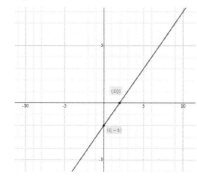

2) $y = -3x + 2$

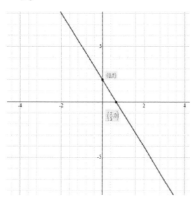

3) $x + y = 0$

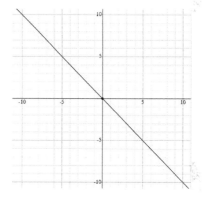

4) $x + y = -3$

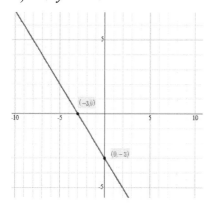

5) $2x + 3y = -4$

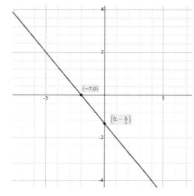

6) $y - 3x + 6 = 0$

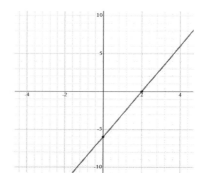

WWW.MathNotion.Com

Algebra 2

Graphing Linear Inequalities

1) $y > 4x - 5$

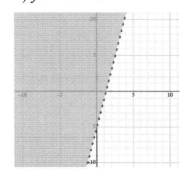

2) $y < 2x + 4$

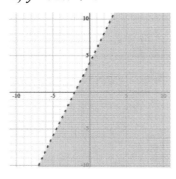

3) $y \leq -5x - 2$

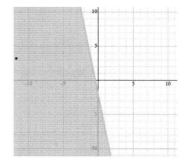

4) $4y \geq 12 + 4x$

5) $-12y < 3x - 24$

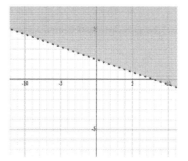

6) $5y \geq -15x + 10$

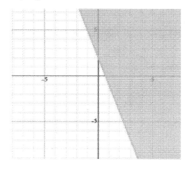

Writing Linear Equations

1) $y = 14x - 33$
2) $y = x + 9$
3) $y = -4x + 47$
4) $y = x - 4$
5) $y = 2x - 31$
6) $y = 9x - 43$
7) $y = -2x + 24$
8) $y = -3x + 1$

9) $y = -2x + 5$
10) $y = -2x + 6$
11) $y = 5x - 18$
12) $y = 14x - 122$
13) $y = 13x + 52$
14) $y = x + 10$
15) $y = -5x + 58$
16) $y = -5x + 5$

17) $y = 6x + 12$
18) $y = -11x - 4$
19) $y = -3x + 17$
20) $y = -5x - 11$
21) $y = -10x - 30$
22) $y = 8x + 7$

Find the value of b

1) -7
2) 11
3) 4
4) 3

Write an equation from a graph

1) $y = 2x + 4$
2) $y = 3x + 5$
3) $y = 5x$
4) $y = 2x + 5$

Algebra 2

Graphing horizontal and vertical lines

1) $y = 3$

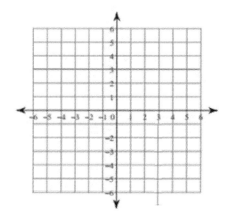

2) $y = -1$ (it is on x axes)

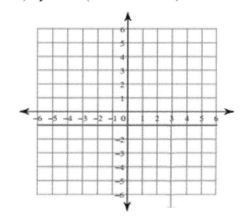

3) $x = 0$

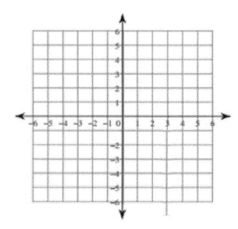

4) $x = 3$

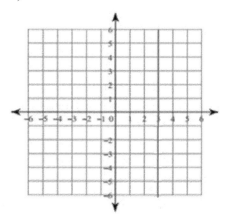

Rate of change

1) 27   2) −12   3) 7

x–intercept and y–intercept

1) $y - \text{intercept} = 5$ $x - \text{intercept} = 3$

2) $y - \text{intercept} = 8$ $x - \text{intercept} = -8$

3) $y - \text{intercept} = -16$ $x - \text{intercept} = 4$

4) $y - \text{intercept} = -2$ $x - \text{intercept} = -2$

5) $y - \text{intercept} = -\frac{7}{3}$ $x - \text{intercept} = \frac{7}{4}$

6) $y - \text{intercept} = -\frac{10}{7}$ $x - \text{intercept} = 2$

7) $y - \text{intercept} = -\frac{8}{3}$ $x - \text{intercept} = -\frac{2}{7}$

8) $y - \text{intercept} = \text{undefind}$ $x - \text{intercept} = 7$

Algebra 2

9) y – intercept = 6   x – intercept = undefind

10) y – intercept = 5   x – intercept = 15

Slope–intercept form

1) $y = 14x + 6$

2) $y = -7x - 12$

3) $y = -\frac{1}{2}x + 3$

4) $y = -\frac{5}{3}x - \frac{14}{3}$

5) $y = \frac{x}{3} - 4$

6) $y = \frac{3}{2}x + \frac{1}{2}$

7) $y = 2x + 4$

8) $y = \frac{7}{4}x + \frac{25}{4}$

9) $y = 6x - 9$

10) $y = -4x + 5$

11) $y = 6x + 9$

12) $y = -2x - 3$

13) $y = -x - 2$

14) $y = x + 7$

15) $y = \frac{2}{3}x - 5$

16) $y = -\frac{1}{3}x - \frac{5}{3}$

Point–slope form

1) $m = 2, (-3, 0)$

2) $m = \frac{1}{3}, (1, -4)$

3) $m = -\frac{3}{2}, (0, -3)$

4) $m = \frac{1}{2}, (2, 3)$

5) $m = \frac{4}{10}, (-3, -2)$

6) $m = -3, (0, 8)$

7) $m = -3, (8, 12)$

8) $m = 0, (0, -14)$

9) $m = 2, (-5, -18)$

10) $m = -8, (-3, 17)$

11) $y + 3 = 4(x - 2)$

12) $y - 4 = \frac{1}{5}(x + 7)$

13) $y + 6 = -2x$

14) $y - b = m(x + a)$

15) $y - 1 = 3(x + 9)$

16) $y = -5(x - 3)$

17) $y - 11 = \frac{1}{3}(x + 4)$

18) $y - 11 = 0$

19) $y - 3 = \frac{1}{5}\left(x + \frac{1}{3}\right)$

20) $y = -3x$

Equation of parallel or perpendicular line.

1) $y = -\frac{1}{3}x - 2\frac{1}{3}$

2) $y = x + 5$

3) $y = \frac{5}{2}x + 5$

4) $y = \frac{4}{3}x$

5) $y = 10$

6) $y = -5x + 7$

7) $y = \frac{4}{5}x + \frac{3}{5}$

8) $y = \frac{8}{5}x + \frac{41}{5}$

9) $y = -\frac{2}{5}x - \frac{4}{5}$

10) $y = -\frac{2}{5}x - 7$

11) $y = \frac{4}{3}x - \frac{10}{3}$

12) $y = -2x - \frac{1}{15}$

13) $x = 2$

14) $y = -2$

15) $y = -2x - 3$

16) $y = \frac{1}{6}x + \frac{3}{10}$

17) $y = -\frac{3}{5}x - 6$

18) $y = -x - 2$

Algebra 2

19) $y = -\frac{3}{7}x - \frac{16}{7}$ 20) $y = -\frac{1}{8}x$

Graphing Absolute Value Equations

1) $y = |x + 4|$ 2) $y = |x - 1|$ 3) $y = -|x| - 1$

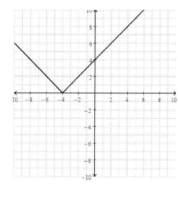 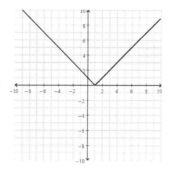 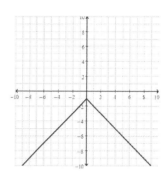

4) $y = |x - 2|$ 5) $y = -|x - 2|$ 6) $y = -2|2x + 2| + 4$

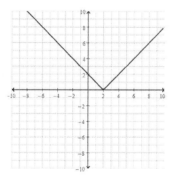 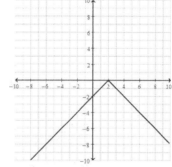 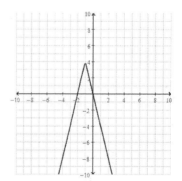

Algebra 2

Chapter 2 :

System of Equations

Topics that you'll practice in this chapter:

- ✓ Systems of Equations
- ✓ Systems of Equations Word Problems
- ✓ Three Variable System of Equations

"If A is a success in life, then A equals x plus y plus z. Work is x; y is play; and z is keeping your mouth shut"
— *Albert Einstein*

Algebra 2

Solving Systems of Equations by Substitution

✎ **Solve each system of equation by substitution.**

1) $-x + 3y = -6$
$x - 2y = 7$

2) $4x + 2y = -4$
$-x - 2y = 5$

3) $2x + 3y = -4$
$3x - y = 8$

4) $y = -2x + 3$
$2x - y = -5$

5) $4x = 8$
$5y = 3x + 4$

6) $4x + 3y = 5$
$2x + y = -8$

7) $3x + 2y = 1$
$x + y = -6$

8) $3y = x + 2$
$2x - y = -4$

WWW.MathNotion.Com   29

Algebra 2

Solving Systems of Equations by Elimination

✎ Solve each system of equation by elimination.

1) $-4x + y = -4$

   $-y = -3x + 3$

2) $-x - 3y = -1$

   $x - 2y = 6$

3) $2x - y = 5$

   $-x + 3y = -5$

4) $x - y = -12$

   $-2x - 3y = 4$

5) $7x + 2y = -15$

   $3x - y = -12$

6) $2x - 3y = -8$

   $x + 2y = 10$

7) $-3x + 15y = -3$

   $2x - 3y = 9$

8) $3x - 4y = -6$

   $6x + 5y = -12$

Algebra 2

Systems of Equations Word Problems

✎ **Find the answer for each word problem.**

1) Tickets to a movie cost $4 for adults and $3 for students. A group of friends purchased 8 tickets for $31.00. How many adults ticket did they buy? ____

2) At a store, Eva bought two shirts and five hats for $77.00. Nicole bought three same shirts and four same hats for $84.00. What is the price of each shirt? _____

3) A farmhouse shelters 18 animals, some are pigs, and some are ducks. Altogether there are 66 legs. How many pigs are there? _____

4) A class of 214 students went on a field trip. They took 36 vehicles, some cars and some buses. If each car holds 5 students and each bus hold 22 students, how many buses did they take? _____

5) A theater is selling tickets for a performance. Mr. Smith purchased 5 senior tickets and 3 child tickets for $105 for his friends and family. Mr. Jackson purchased 3 senior tickets and 5 child tickets for $79. What is the price of a senior ticket? $_____

6) The difference of two numbers is 10. Their sum is 20. What is the bigger number? $_____

7) The sum of the digits of a certain two-digit number is 7. Reversing its digits increase the number by 9. What is the number? _____

8) The difference of two numbers is 11. Their sum is 25. What are the numbers? _____

9) The length of a rectangle is 5 meters greater than 2 times the width. The perimeter of rectangle is 28 meters. What is the length of the rectangle? _____

10) Jim has 25 nickels and dimes totaling $1.80. How many nickels does he have? _____

WWW.MathNotion.Com

Algebra 2

Three Variables System of Equations

✎ **Solve each system of equations.**

1) $x = 3y - 3z + 8$ $x = \underline{}$

   $z = 4x + 5y - 14$ $y = \underline{}$

   $3y + 2z = 14$ $z = \underline{}$

2) $6x - 6y = -12$ $x = \underline{}$

   $2z = -6x - 6y + 18$ $y = \underline{}$

   $-8x + 10y + 2z = 16$ $z = \underline{}$

3) $4x - 8z = 40$ $x = \underline{}$

   $-6x + 2y - 8z = 40$ $y = \underline{}$

   $-8x + 4y + 6z = -30$ $z = \underline{}$

4) $2x - 4y + 2z = -12$ $x = \underline{}$

   $2x + 10z = -24$ $y = \underline{}$

   $-2x + 12y + 8z = 6$ $z = \underline{}$

5) $x - y - 2z = -6$ $x = \underline{}$

   $3x + 2y = -25$ $y = \underline{}$

   $-4x + y - z = 12$ $z = \underline{}$

6) $6x - y + 3z = -9$ $x = \underline{}$

   $5x + 5y - 5z = 20$ $y = \underline{}$

   $3x - y + 4z = -5$ $z = \underline{}$

7) $-5x + 3y + 6z = 4$ $x = \underline{}$

   $-3x + y + 5z = -5$ $y = \underline{}$

   $-4x + 2y + z = 13$ $z = \underline{}$

8) $-6x + 5y + 2z = -11$ $x = \underline{}$

   $-2x + y + 4z = -9$ $y = \underline{}$

   $4x - 5y + 5z = -4$ $z = \underline{}$

9) $4x + 4y + z = 24$ $x = \underline{}$

   $2x - 4y + z = 0$ $y = \underline{}$

   $5x - 4y - 5z = 12$ $z = \underline{}$

10) $-10x + 10y + 6z = -46$ $x = \underline{}$

    $-10x + 6y - 6z = -22$ $y = \underline{}$

    $-12x + 12z = -24$ $z = \underline{}$

WWW.MathNotion.Com

Algebra 2

Answers of Worksheets

Solving Systems of Equations by Substitution

1) (9, 1)
2) $(\frac{1}{3}, -\frac{8}{3})$
3) $(\frac{20}{11}, -\frac{28}{11})$
4) $(-\frac{1}{2}, 4)$
5) (2, 2)
6) $(-\frac{29}{2}, 21)$
7) (13, −19)
8) (−2, 0)

Solving Systems of Equations by Elimination

1) (1, 0)
2) (4, −1)
3) (2, −1)
4) (−8, 4)
5) (−3, 3)
6) (2, 4)
7) (6, 1)
8) (−2, 0)

Systems of Equations Word Problems

1) 7
2) $16
3) 15
4) 2
5) $18
6) 15
7) 34
8) 18, 7
9) 11 meters
10) 14

Three variable System of equations

1) (2, 2, 4)
2) (1, 3, −3)
3) (0, 0, −5)
4) (3, 3, −3)
5) (−5, −5, 3)
6) (−1, 6, 1)
7) (−2, 4, −3)
8) (4, 3, −1)
9) (4, 2, 0)
10) (1, −3, −1)

Algebra 2

Chapter 3 :
Radicals Expressions

Topics that you'll practice in this chapter:

- ✓ Simplifying Radical Expressions
- ✓ Adding and Subtracting Radical Expressions
- ✓ Simplifying Radical Expressions Involving Fractions
- ✓ Multiplying Radical Expressions

"To be radical is to grasp things by the root."

— *Karl Marx,*

Algebra 2

Simplifying Radical Expressions

✎ **Simplify.**

1) $\sqrt{13x^2} =$

2) $\sqrt{75x^2} =$

3) $\sqrt[3]{27a} =$

4) $\sqrt{64x^5} =$

5) $\sqrt{216a} =$

6) $\sqrt[3]{63w^3} =$

7) $\sqrt{192x} =$

8) $\sqrt{125v} =$

9) $\sqrt[3]{128x^2} =$

10) $\sqrt{100x^9} =$

11) $\sqrt{16x^4} =$

12) $\sqrt[3]{500a^5} =$

13) $\sqrt{242} =$

14) $\sqrt{392p^3} =$

15) $\sqrt{8m^6} =$

16) $\sqrt{198x^3y^3} =$

17) $\sqrt{121x^5y^5} =$

18) $\sqrt{16a^6b^3} =$

19) $\sqrt{90x^5y^7} =$

20) $\sqrt[3]{64y^2x^6} =$

21) $10\sqrt{16x^4} =$

22) $6\sqrt{81x^2} =$

23) $\sqrt[3]{56x^2y^6} =$

24) $\sqrt[3]{1,000x^5y^7} =$

25) $8\sqrt{50a} =$

26) $\sqrt[4]{625x^8y} =$

27) $\sqrt{24x^4y^5r^3} =$

28) $5\sqrt{36x^4y^5z^8} =$

29) $3\sqrt[3]{343x^9y^7} =$

30) $5\sqrt{81a^5b^2c^9} =$

31) $\sqrt[4]{625x^8y^{16}} =$

WWW.MathNotion.Com

Algebra 2

Adding and Subtracting Radical Expressions

✏️ **Simplify.**

1) $\sqrt{2} + \sqrt{8} =$

2) $3\sqrt{50} + 4\sqrt{2} =$

3) $2\sqrt{12} - 4\sqrt{3} =$

4) $5\sqrt{32} - 5\sqrt{2} =$

5) $3\sqrt{75} - 5\sqrt{3} =$

6) $-\sqrt{72} - 4\sqrt{2} =$

7) $-7\sqrt{16} - 4\sqrt{25} =$

8) $8\sqrt{24} + 2\sqrt{6} =$

9) $10\sqrt{49} - 7\sqrt{100} =$

10) $-7\sqrt{5} + 9\sqrt{45} =$

11) $-15\sqrt{12} + 14\sqrt{48} =$

12) $20\sqrt{4} - 2\sqrt{25} =$

13) $-2\sqrt{20} + 7\sqrt{5} =$

14) $8\sqrt{7} - 2\sqrt{63} =$

15) $5\sqrt{44} + 3\sqrt{11} =$

16) $3\sqrt{27} - 5\sqrt{48} =$

17) $\sqrt{144} - \sqrt{81} =$

18) $3\sqrt{20} - 6\sqrt{5} =$

19) $-2\sqrt{7} + 8\sqrt{28} =$

20) $3\sqrt{75} - 2\sqrt{3} =$

21) $5\sqrt{27} - 3\sqrt{3} =$

22) $-7\sqrt{30} + 6\sqrt{120} =$

23) $-7\sqrt{24} - 2\sqrt{6} =$

24) $-\sqrt{32x} + 4\sqrt{2x} =$

25) $\sqrt{7y^2} + y\sqrt{112} =$

26) $\sqrt{45mn^2} + 2n\sqrt{5m} =$

27) $-4\sqrt{12a} - 4\sqrt{3a} =$

28) $-5\sqrt{15ab} - 2\sqrt{60ab} =$

29) $\sqrt{45x^2y} + x\sqrt{20y} =$

30) $2\sqrt{7a} + 4\sqrt{63a} =$

WWW.MathNotion.Com

Algebra 2

Multiplying Radical Expressions

✎ **Simplify.**

1) $\sqrt{5} \times \sqrt{5} =$

2) $\sqrt{5} \times \sqrt{10} =$

3) $\sqrt{3} \times \sqrt{12} =$

4) $\sqrt{49} \times \sqrt{47} =$

5) $\sqrt{7} \times -2\sqrt{28} =$

6) $3\sqrt{15} \times \sqrt{5} =$

7) $4\sqrt{72} \times \sqrt{2} =$

8) $\sqrt{5} \times -\sqrt{49} =$

9) $\sqrt{55} \times \sqrt{11} =$

10) $7\sqrt{42} \times 2\sqrt{216} =$

11) $\sqrt{45}(5 + \sqrt{5}) =$

12) $\sqrt{13x^2} \times \sqrt{13x^3} =$

13) $-2\sqrt{27} \times \sqrt{3} =$

14) $2\sqrt{13x^4} \times \sqrt{13x^4} =$

15) $\sqrt{14x^3} \times \sqrt{7x^2} =$

16) $-8\sqrt{5x} \times \sqrt{7x^5} =$

17) $-2\sqrt{16x^5} \times 4\sqrt{8x^3} =$

18) $-4\sqrt{32}(8 + \sqrt{32}) =$

19) $\sqrt{32x}(10 - \sqrt{2x}) =$

20) $\sqrt{2x}(8\sqrt{x^5} + \sqrt{8}) =$

21) $\sqrt{20r}(5 + \sqrt{5}) =$

22) $-4\sqrt{7x} \times 3\sqrt{14x^5} =$

23) $-2\sqrt{12x} \times 3\sqrt{2x}$

24) $-\sqrt{7v^3}(-3\sqrt{42v}) =$

25) $(\sqrt{11} - 5)(\sqrt{11} + 5) =$

26) $(-3\sqrt{5} + 3)(\sqrt{5} - 4) =$

27) $(4 - 6\sqrt{3})(-6 + \sqrt{3}) =$

28) $(8 - 3\sqrt{5})(7 - \sqrt{5}) =$

29) $(-1 - \sqrt{3x})(4 + \sqrt{3x}) =$

30) $(-5 + 2\sqrt{7r})(-5 + \sqrt{7r}) =$

31) $(-\sqrt{7n} + 1)(-\sqrt{7} - 5) =$

32) $(-3 + \sqrt{3})(5 - 2\sqrt{3x}) =$

WWW.MathNotion.Com

Algebra 2

Simplifying Radical Expressions Involving Fractions

✎ **Simplify.**

1) $\dfrac{\sqrt{5}}{\sqrt{3}} =$

2) $\dfrac{\sqrt{18}}{\sqrt{45}} =$

3) $\dfrac{\sqrt{10}}{5\sqrt{2}} =$

4) $\dfrac{13}{\sqrt{3}} =$

5) $\dfrac{12\sqrt{5r}}{\sqrt{m^5}} =$

6) $\dfrac{11\sqrt{2}}{\sqrt{k}} =$

7) $\dfrac{6\sqrt{20x^3}}{\sqrt{16x}} =$

8) $\dfrac{\sqrt{14x^3y^4}}{\sqrt{7x^4y^3}} =$

9) $\dfrac{1}{1-\sqrt{5}} =$

10) $\dfrac{1-8\sqrt{a}}{\sqrt{11a}} =$

11) $\dfrac{\sqrt{a}}{\sqrt{a}+\sqrt{b}} =$

12) $\dfrac{1-\sqrt{5}}{2-\sqrt{6}} =$

13) $\dfrac{4+\sqrt{7}}{3-\sqrt{8}} =$

14) $\dfrac{5}{-3-3\sqrt{3}} =$

15) $\dfrac{7}{2-\sqrt{5}} =$

16) $\dfrac{\sqrt{7}-\sqrt{3}}{\sqrt{3}-\sqrt{7}} =$

17) $\dfrac{\sqrt{5}+\sqrt{7}}{\sqrt{7}-\sqrt{5}} =$

18) $\dfrac{2\sqrt{2}-\sqrt{3}}{3\sqrt{2}+\sqrt{5}} =$

19) $\dfrac{\sqrt{11}+5\sqrt{3}}{4-\sqrt{11}} =$

20) $\dfrac{\sqrt{5}+\sqrt{3}}{2-\sqrt{3}} =$

21) $\dfrac{\sqrt{32a^7b^4}}{\sqrt{2ab^3}} =$

22) $\dfrac{10\sqrt{21x^5}}{5\sqrt{x^3}} =$

WWW.MathNotion.Com

Algebra 2

Answers of Worksheets

Simplifying radical expressions

1) $x\sqrt{13}$
2) $5x\sqrt{3}$
3) $3\sqrt[3]{a}$
4) $8x^2\sqrt{x}$
5) $6\sqrt{6a}$
6) $w\sqrt[3]{63}$
7) $8\sqrt{3x}$
8) $5\sqrt{5v}$
9) $4\sqrt[3]{2x^2}$
10) $10x^4\sqrt{x}$
11) $4x^2$
12) $5a\sqrt[3]{4a^2}$
13) $11\sqrt{2}$
14) $14p\sqrt{2p}$
15) $2m^3\sqrt{2}$
16) $3x.y\sqrt{22xy}$
17) $11x^2y^2\sqrt{xy}$
18) $4a^3b\sqrt{b}$
19) $3x^2y^3\sqrt{10xy}$
20) $4x^2\sqrt[3]{y^2}$
21) $40x^2$
22) $54x$
23) $2y^2\sqrt[3]{7x^2}$
24) $10xy^2\sqrt[3]{x^2y}$
25) $40\sqrt{2a}$
26) $5x^2\sqrt[4]{y}$
27) $2x^2y^2r\sqrt{6yr}$
28) $30x^2y^2z^4\sqrt{y}$
29) $21x^3y^2\sqrt[3]{y}$
30) $45a^2bc^4\sqrt{ac}$
31) $5x^2y^4$

Adding and subtracting radical expressions

1) $3\sqrt{2}$
2) $19\sqrt{2}$
3) 0
4) $15\sqrt{2}$
5) $10\sqrt{3}$
6) $-10\sqrt{2}$
7) -48
8) $18\sqrt{6}$
9) 0
10) $20\sqrt{5}$
11) $26\sqrt{3}$
12) 30
13) $3\sqrt{5}$
14) $2\sqrt{7}$
15) $13\sqrt{11}$
16) $-11\sqrt{3}$
17) 3
18) 0
19) $14\sqrt{7}$
20) $13\sqrt{3}$
21) $12\sqrt{3}$
22) $5\sqrt{30}$
23) $-16\sqrt{6}$
24) 0
25) $5y\sqrt{7}$
26) $5n\sqrt{5m}$
27) $-12\sqrt{3a}$
28) $-9\sqrt{15ab}$
29) $5x\sqrt{5y}$
30) $14\sqrt{7a}$

Multiplying radical expressions

1) 5
2) $5\sqrt{2}$
3) 6
4) $7\sqrt{47}$
5) -28
6) $15\sqrt{3}$
7) 48
8) $-5\sqrt{7}$
9) $11\sqrt{5}$

WWW.MathNotion.Com

Algebra 2

10) $504\sqrt{7}$

11) $15\sqrt{5} + 15$

12) $13x^2\sqrt{x}$

13) -18

14) $26x^4$

15) $7x^2\sqrt{2x}$

16) $-8x^3\sqrt{35}$

17) $-64x^4\sqrt{2}$

18) $-128\sqrt{2} - 128$

19) $40\sqrt{2x} - 8x$

20) $8x^3\sqrt{2} + 4\sqrt{x}$

21) $10\sqrt{5r} + 10\sqrt{r}$

22) $-84x^3\sqrt{2}$

23) $-12\sqrt{6}x$

24) $21v^2\sqrt{6}$

25) -14

26) $15\sqrt{5} - 27$

27) $40\sqrt{3} - 42$

28) $71 - 29\sqrt{5}$

29) $-3x - 5\sqrt{3x} - 4$

30) $14r - 15\sqrt{7r} + 25$

31) $7\sqrt{n} + 5\sqrt{7n} - \sqrt{7} - 5$

32) $-15 + 6\sqrt{3x} + 5\sqrt{3} - 6\sqrt{x}$

Simplifying radical expressions involving fractions

1) $\frac{\sqrt{15}}{3}$

2) $\frac{9\sqrt{10}}{45} = \frac{\sqrt{10}}{5}$

3) $\frac{\sqrt{20}}{10} = \frac{\sqrt{5}}{5}$

4) $\frac{13\sqrt{3}}{3}$

5) $\frac{12\sqrt{5mr}}{m^3}$

6) $\frac{11\sqrt{2k}}{k}$

7) $3x\sqrt{5}$

8) $\frac{\sqrt{2x}}{xy}$

9) $\frac{-1-\sqrt{5}}{4}$

10) $\frac{\sqrt{11a} - 8a\sqrt{11}}{11a}$

11) $\frac{a - \sqrt{ab}}{a - b}$

12) $\frac{\sqrt{30} + 2\sqrt{5} - \sqrt{6} - 2}{2}$

13) $12 + 8\sqrt{2} + 3\sqrt{7} + 2\sqrt{14}$

14) $-\frac{5(\sqrt{3} - 1)}{6}$

15) $-14 - 7\sqrt{5}$

16) -1

17) $6 + \sqrt{35}$

18) $\frac{12 - 2\sqrt{10} - 3\sqrt{6} + \sqrt{15}}{13}$

19) $\frac{4\sqrt{11} + 11 + 20\sqrt{3} + 5\sqrt{33}}{5}$

20) $2\sqrt{5} + 3 + \sqrt{15} + 2\sqrt{3}$

21) $4a^3\sqrt{b}$

22) $2x\sqrt{21}$

Algebra 2

Chapter 4 :
Functions Operations and Quadratic

Topics that you'll practice in this chapter:

- ✓ Relations and Functions
- ✓ Evaluating Function
- ✓ Adding and Subtracting Functions
- ✓ Multiplying and Dividing Functions
- ✓ Composition of Functions
- ✓ Quadratic Equation
- ✓ Solving Quadratic Equations
- ✓ Quadratic Formula and the Discriminant
- ✓ Quadratic Inequalities
- ✓ Graphing Quadratic Functions
- ✓ Domain and Range of Radical Functions
- ✓ Solving Radical Equations

It's fine to work on any problem, so long as it generates interesting mathematics along the way – even if you don't solve it at the end of the day." – Andrew Wiles

Algebra 2

Relations and Functions

✎ State the domain and range of each relation. Then determine whether each relation is a function.

1)
Function:
....
Domain:
....
Range:
....

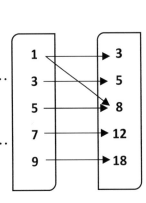

2)
Function:
....
Domain:
....
Range:
....

x	y
3	4
0	1
−2	−3
6	−3
8	2

3)
Function:
....
Domain:
....
Range:
....

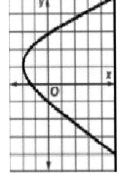

4) $\{(1, -2), (4, -1), (0, 5), (4, 0), (3, 8)\}$
Function:
....
Domain:
....
Range:
....

5)
Function:
....
Domain:
....
Range:
....

6)
Function:
....
Domain:
....
Range:
....

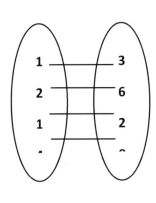

Algebra 2

Evaluating Function

✎ **Write each of following in function notation.**

1) $h = -8x + 3$

2) $k = 2a - 14$

3) $d = 11t$

4) $y = \frac{5}{12}x - \frac{7}{12}$

5) $m = 24n - 210$

6) $c = p^2 - 5p + 10$

✎ **Evaluate each function.**

7) $f(x) = 2x - 7$, find $f(-3)$

8) $g(x) = \frac{1}{9}x + 12$, find $f(18)$

9) $h(x) = -4x + 9$, find $f(3)$

10) $f(x) = -x + 19$, find $f(-3)$

11) $f(a) = 7a - 12$, find $f(3)$

12) $h(x) = 14 - 3x$, find $f(-4)$

13) $g(n) = 6n - 10$, find $f(2)$

14) $f(x) = -11x - 4$, find $f(-1)$

15) $k(n) = -20 - 3.5n$, find $f(2)$

16) $f(x) = -0.7x + 3.3$, find $f(-7)$

17) $g(n) = \frac{11n+8}{n}$, find $g(2)$

18) $g(n) = \sqrt{3n} + 12$, find $g(3)$

19) $h(x) = x^{-2} - 7$, find $h(\frac{1}{9})$

20) $h(n) = n^{-3} + 11$, find $h(\frac{1}{4})$

21) $h(n) = n^3 - 2$, find $h(\frac{1}{2})$

22) $h(n) = n^2 - 4$, find $h(-\frac{1}{3})$

23) $h(n) = 4n^2 - 13$, find $h(-5)$

24) $h(n) = -2n^3 - 6n$, find $h(2)$

25) $g(n) = \sqrt{16n^2} - \sqrt{n}$, find $g(4)$

26) $h(a) = \frac{-14a+9}{3a}$, find $h(-b)$

27) $k(a) = 12a - 14$, find $k(a - 3)$

28) $h(x) = \frac{1}{9}x + 18$, find $h(-18x)$

29) $h(x) = 8x^2 + 16$, find $h(\frac{x}{2})$

30) $h(x) = x^4 - 20$, find $h(-2x)$

WWW.MathNotion.Com

Algebra 2

Adding and Subtracting Functions

✍ **Perform the indicated operation.**

1) $f(x) = 2x + 3$

   $g(x) = x + 7$

   Find $(f - g)(2)$

2) $g(a) = -5a - 8$

   $f(a) = -3a - 5$

   Find $(g - f)(-2)$

3) $h(t) = 4t + 3$

   $g(t) = 4t + 7$

   Find $(h - g)(t)$

4) $g(a) = -6a - 10$

   $f(a) = 3a^2 + 9$

   Find $(g - f)(x)$

5) $g(x) = \frac{5}{6}x - 23$

   $h(x) = \frac{5}{12}x + 25$

   Find $g(12) - h(12)$

6) $h(x) = \sqrt{3x} - 2$

   $g(x) = \sqrt{3x} + 5$

   Find $(h + g)(12)$

7) $f(x) = x^{-1}$

   $g(x) = x^2 + \frac{5}{x}$

   Find $(f - g)(-3)$

8) $h(n) = n^2 + 2$

   $g(n) = -4n + 6$

   Find $(h - g)(2a)$

9) $g(x) = -2x^2 - 5 - 4x$

   $f(x) = 7 + 2x$

   Find $(g - f)(3x)$

10) $g(t) = 11t - 4$

    $f(t) = -2t^2 + 5$

    Find $(g + f)(-t)$

11) $f(x) = 8x + 9$

    $g(x) = -5x^2 + 3x$

    Find $(f - g)(-x^2)$

12) $f(x) = -3x^4 - 5x$

    $g(x) = 2x^4 + 5x + 22$

    Find $(f + g)(3x^2)$

WWW.MathNotion.Com

Algebra 2

Multiplying and Dividing Functions

✎ **Perform the indicated operation.**

1) $g(x) = -2x - 1$
$f(x) = 4x + 3$
Find $(g.f)(2)$

2) $f(x) = 5x$
$h(x) = -2x + 3$
Find $(f.h)(-2)$

3) $g(a) = 5a - 2$
$h(a) = 2a - 3$
Find $(g.h)(-3)$

4) $f(x) = 2x - 7$
$h(x) = x - 5$
Find $\left(\dfrac{f}{h}\right)(4)$

5) $f(x) = 8a^2$
$g(x) = 3 + 2a$
Find $\left(\dfrac{f}{g}\right)(2)$

6) $g(a) = \sqrt{4a} + 2$
$f(a) = (-a)^4 + 1$
Find $\left(\dfrac{g}{f}\right)(1)$

7) $g(t) = t^3 + 1$
$h(t) = 5t - 2$
Find $(g.h)(-2)$

8) $g(n) = n^2 + 2n - 4$
$h(n) = -5n + 3$
Find $(g.h)(1)$

9) $g(a) = (a - 3)^2$
$f(a) = a^2 + 4$
Find $\left(\dfrac{g}{f}\right)(3)$

10) $g(x) = -3x^2 + \dfrac{4}{5}x + 9$
$f(x) = x^2 - 24$
Find $\left(\dfrac{g}{f}\right)(5)$

11) $f(x) = 2x^3 - 5x^2 + 1$
$g(x) = 3x - 1$
Find $(f.g)(x)$

12) $f(x) = 5x - 2$
$g(x) = x^3 - 2x$
Find $(f.g)(x^2)$

Algebra 2

Composition of Functions

Using $f(x) = 2x - 5$ and $g(x) = -2x$, find:

1) $f(g(2)) =$

2) $f(g(-1)) =$

3) $g(f(-4)) =$

4) $g(f(5)) =$

5) $f(g(3)) =$

6) $g(f(0)) =$

Using $f(x) = -\frac{1}{4}x + \frac{3}{4}$ and $g(x) = 2x^2$, find:

7) $g(f(-2)) =$

8) $g(f(4)) =$

9) $g(g(1)) =$

10) $f(f(1)) =$

11) $g(f(-4)) =$

12) $f(g(x)) =$

Using $f(x) = -2x + 2$ and $g(x) = x + 1$, find:

13) $g(f(1)) =$

14) $f(f(0)) =$

15) $f(g(-1)) =$

16) $f(g(-3)) =$

17) $g(f(2)) =$

18) $f(g(x)) =$

Using $f(x) = \sqrt{x + 9}$ and $g(x) = x - 9$, find:

19) $f(g(9)) =$

20) $g(f(-9)) =$

21) $f(g(4)) =$

22) $f(f(7)) =$

23) $g(f(-5)) =$

24) $g(g(0)) =$

WWW.MathNotion.Com

Algebra 2

Quadratic Equation

✎ **Multiply.**

1) $(x-4)(x+6) = $ _____

2) $(x+5)(x+7) = $ _____

3) $(x-6)(x+8) = $ _____

4) $(x+2)(x-9) = $ _____

5) $(x-7)(x-8) = $ _____

6) $(3x+2)(x-3) = $ _____

7) $(4x-3)(x+2) = $ _____

8) $(4x-5)(x+1) = $ _____

9) $(7x+1)(x-6) = $ _____

10) $(5x+1)(3x-3) = $ _____

✎ **Factor each expression.**

11) $x^2 - 2x - 8 = $ _____

12) $x^2 + 8x + 15 = $ _____

13) $x^2 - 2x - 24 = $ _____

14) $x^2 - 10x + 21 = $ _____

15) $x^2 + 10x + 21 = $ _____

16) $4x^2 + 9x + 5 = $ _____

17) $5x^2 + 13x - 6 = $ _____

18) $5x^2 + 17x - 12 = $ _____

19) $2x^2 + 7x + 5 = $ _____

20) $9x^2 - 21x + 6 = $ _____

✎ **Calculate each equation.**

21) $(x+6)(x-3) = 0$

22) $(x+1)(x+8) = 0$

23) $(3x+6)(x+5) = 0$

24) $(2x-2)(4x+8) = 0$

25) $x^2 + x + 10 = 22$

26) $x^2 + 11x + 36 = 12$

27) $2x^2 + 9x + 9 = 5$

28) $x^2 + 3x - 24 = 4$

29) $5x^2 + 5x - 40 = 20$

30) $8x^2 + 8x = 48$

Algebra 2

Solving Quadratic Equations

✎ **Solve each equation by factoring or using the quadratic formula.**

1) $(x + 9)(x - 1) = 0$

2) $(x + 7)(x + 6) = 0$

3) $(x - 8)(x + 3) = 0$

4) $(x - 6)(x - 4) = 0$

5) $(x + 2)(x + 12) = 0$

6) $(5x + 4)(x + 7) = 0$

7) $(6x + 1)(4x + 5) = 0$

8) $(2x + 7)(x + 8) = 0$

9) $(x + 6)(3x + 15) = 0$

10) $(12x + 2)(x + 8) = 0$

11) $x^2 = 8x$

12) $x^2 - 16 = 0$

13) $3x^2 + 6 = 9x$

14) $-2x^2 - 8 = 10x$

15) $5x^2 + 40x = 45$

16) $x^2 + 10x = 24$

17) $x^2 + 6x = 16$

18) $x^2 + 9x = -18$

19) $x^2 + 13x = -36$

20) $x^2 + 3x - 15 = 5x$

21) $x^2 + 8x + 7 = -8$

22) $3x^2 - 11x = -9 + x$

23) $10x^2 + 3 = 27x - 15$

24) $7x^2 - 6x + 8 = 8$

25) $2x^2 - 12 = -3x + 2$

26) $10x^2 - 26x - 3 = -15$

27) $3x^2 + 21 = -16x + 5$

28) $x^2 + 15x - 10 = -66$

29) $3x^2 - 8x - 8 = 4 + x$

30) $2x^2 + 6x - 24 = 12$

31) $3x^2 - 33x + 54 = -18$

32) $-10x^2 - 15x - 9 = -9 - 27x^2$

WWW.MathNotion.Com

Algebra 2

Quadratic Formula and the Discriminant

✏️ **Find the value of the discriminant of each quadratic equation.**

1) $3x(x - 8) = 0$

2) $2x^2 + 6x - 4 = 0$

3) $x^2 + 6x + 7 = 0$

4) $x^2 - x + 3 = 0$

5) $x^2 + 4x - 3 = 0$

6) $2x^2 + 6x - 10 = 0$

7) $3x^2 + 7x + 5 = 0$

8) $x^2 - 6x - 4 = 0$

9) $2x^2 + 8x + 3 = 0$

10) $x^2 + 7x - 5 = 0$

11) $5x^2 + 2x - 3 = 0$

12) $-3x^2 - 11x + 4 = 0$

13) $-6x^2 - 12x + 8 = 0$

14) $-x^2 - 9x - 12 = 0$

15) $7x^2 - 6x - 10 = 0$

16) $-4x^2 - 2x + 8 = 0$

17) $5x^2 + 8x - 2 = 0$

18) $6x^2 - 4x = 0$

19) $3x^2 - 5x + 2 = 0$

20) $4x^2 + 9x + 3 = 0$

✏️ **Find the discriminant of each quadratic equation then state the number of real and imaginary solutions.**

21) $-4x^2 - 16 = 16x$

22) $20x^2 = 20x - 5$

23) $-11x^2 - 19x = 26$

24) $22x^2 - 4x + 1 = 18x^2$

25) $-11x^2 = -15x + 8$

26) $3x^2 + 6x + 9 = 6$

27) $13x^2 - 5x - 12 = -26$

28) $-8x^2 - 32x - 25 = 7$

WWW.MathNotion.Com

Algebra 2

Graphing Quadratic Functions

Sketch the graph of each function. Identify the vertex and axis of symmetry.

1) $y = (x + 3)^2 + 2$

2) $y = (x - 3)^2 - 2$

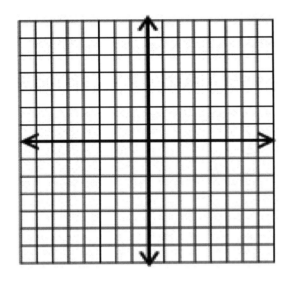
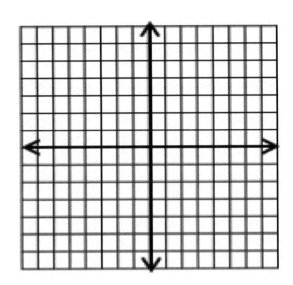

3) $y = 6 - (-x + 4)^2$

4) $y = -3x^2 - 6x + 9$

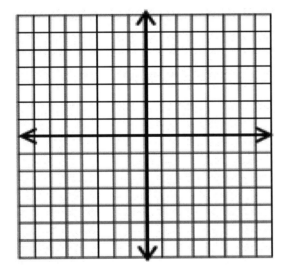
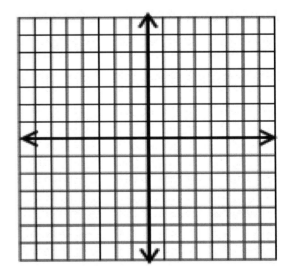

WWW.MathNotion.Com

Algebra 2

Quadratic Inequalities

✎ **Solve each quadratic inequality.**

1) $x^2 - 25 < 0$

2) $-x^2 - 6x - 8 > 0$

3) $5x^2 + 15x + 30 < 0$

4) $x^2 + 8x + 16 > 0$

5) $2x^2 - 18x - 20 \geq 0$

6) $x^2 > -10x - 25$

7) $3x^2 + 2x + 16 \leq 0$

8) $x^2 - 5x - 14 \leq 0$

9) $x^2 - 6x - 7 \geq 0$

10) $2x^2 + 16x - 18 < 0$

11) $x^2 + 6x - 72 > 0$

12) $3x^2 - 3x - 36 > 0$

13) $x^2 - 15x + 64 \leq 0$

14) $2x^2 - 24x + 72 \leq 0$

15) $x^2 - 16x + 63 \geq 0$

16) $x^2 - 16x + 55 \geq 0$

17) $x^2 - 81 \leq 0$

18) $x^2 - 17x + 42 \geq 0$

19) $9x^2 + 14x + 36 \leq 0$

20) $4x^2 - 2x - 24 > 2x^2$

21) $5x^2 - 20x + 20 < 0$

22) $7x^2 - 6x \geq 6x^2 - 5$

23) $5x^2 - 15 > 4x^2 + 2x$

24) $3x^2 - 4x \geq 3x^2 - 9x + 15$

25) $8x^2 + 9x - 54 > 5x^2$

26) $10x^2 + 50x - 60 < 0$

27) $-x^2 + 15x - 57 \geq 0$

28) $-5x^2 + 25x + 30 \leq 0$

29) $5x^2 + 40x + 75 < 0$

30) $9x^2 + 20x + 180 \leq 0$

31) $3x^2 + 2x - 36 \geq -x$

32) $3x^2 + 9x + 9 \leq 6x^2 + 3x$

WWW.MathNotion.Com

Algebra 2

Domain and Range of Radical Functions

✎ **Identify the domain and range of each function.**

1) $y = \sqrt{x+8} - 7$

2) $y = \sqrt[3]{3x-5} - 4$

3) $y = \sqrt{3x-9} + 3$

4) $y = \sqrt[3]{(4x+6)} - 2$

5) $y = 3\sqrt{4x+20} + 6$

6) $y = \sqrt[3]{(5x-2)} - 11$

7) $y = 4\sqrt{9x^2+8} + 3$

8) $y = \sqrt[3]{(7x^2-2)} - 6$

9) $y = 2\sqrt{2x^3+16} - 3$

10) $y = \sqrt[3]{(11x+4)} - 2x$

11) $y = 3\sqrt{-2(4x+8)} + 5$

12) $y = \sqrt[5]{(3x^2-12)} - 6$

13) $y = 3\sqrt{x-5} - 2$

14) $y = \sqrt[3]{6x+9} - 4$

✎ **Sketch the graph of each function.**

15) $y = -3\sqrt{x} + 5$

16) $y = 3\sqrt{x} - 6$

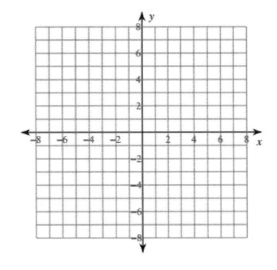
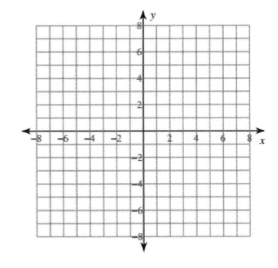

Algebra 2

Solving Radical Equations

✎ **Solve each equation. Remember to check for extraneous solutions.**

1) $\sqrt{a} = 9$

2) $\sqrt{v} = 6$

3) $\sqrt{r} = 4$

4) $8 = 16\sqrt{x}$

5) $\sqrt{x+3} = 18$

6) $6 = \sqrt{x-7}$

7) $4 = \sqrt{r-3}$

8) $\sqrt{x-5} = 7$

9) $12 = \sqrt{x-4}$

10) $\sqrt{m+5} = 8$

11) $7\sqrt{5a} = 35$

12) $6\sqrt{2x} = 48$

13) $2 = \sqrt{6x-32}$

14) $\sqrt{304-4x} = 4$

15) $\sqrt{r+2} - 8 = 6$

16) $-21 = -7\sqrt{r+9}$

17) $60 = 6\sqrt{5v}$

18) $x = \sqrt{40-3x}$

19) $\sqrt{90-27a} = 3a$

20) $\sqrt{-8n+88} = 4$

21) $\sqrt{15r-5} = 4r-3$

22) $\sqrt{-64+32x} = 4x$

23) $\sqrt{4x+15} = \sqrt{2x+11}$

24) $\sqrt{12v} = \sqrt{15v-21}$

25) $\sqrt{9-x} = \sqrt{x-3}$

26) $\sqrt{6m+34} = \sqrt{8m+34}$

27) $\sqrt{7r+32} = \sqrt{-8-3r}$

28) $\sqrt{4k+10} = \sqrt{2-4k}$

29) $-20\sqrt{x-13} = -40$

30) $\sqrt{90-2x} = \sqrt{\frac{x}{4}}$

Algebra 2

Answers of Worksheets

Relation and Functions

1) No, $D_f = \{1, 3, 5, 7, 9\}$, $R_f = \{3, 5, 8, 12, 18\}$
2) Yes, $D_f = \{3, 0, -2, 6, 8\}$, $R_f = \{4, 1, -3, 2\}$
3) Yes, $D_f = (-\infty, \infty)$, $R_f = \{2, -\infty\}$
4) No, $D_f = \{1, 4, 0, 3\}$, $R_f = \{-2, -1, 5, 0, 8\}$
5) No, $D_f = [-2, \infty)$, $R_f = (-\infty, \infty)$
6) No, $D_f = \{1, 2, 4\}$, $R_f = \{3, 6, 2, 8\}$

Evaluating Function

1) $h(x) = -8x + 3$
2) $k(a) = 2a - 14$
3) $d(t) = 11t$
4) $f(x) = \frac{5}{12}x - \frac{7}{12}$
5) $m(n) = 24n - 210$
6) $c(p) = p^2 - 5p + 10$
7) -13
8) 14
9) -3
10) 22
11) 9
12) 26
13) 2
14) 7
15) -27
16) 8.2
17) 15
18) 15
19) 74
20) 75
21) $-1\frac{7}{8}$
22) $-3\frac{8}{9}$
23) 87
24) -28
25) 14
26) $-\frac{14b+9}{3b}$
27) $12a - 50$
28) $-2x + 18$
29) $2x^2 + 16$
30) $16x^4 - 20$

Adding and Subtracting Functions

1) -2
2) 1
3) -4
4) $-3x^2 - 6x - 19$
5) -43
6) 15
7) $-7\frac{2}{3}$
8) $4a^2 + 8a - 4$
9) $-18x^2 - 18x - 12$
10) $-2t^2 - 11t + 1$
11) $5x^4 - 5x^2 + 9$
12) $-81x^8 + 22$

Multiplying and Dividing Functions

1) -55
2) -70
3) 153
4) -1
5) $4\frac{4}{7}$
6) 2
7) 84
8) 2
9) 0
10) -62

Algebra 2

11) $6x^4 - 17x^3 + 5x^2 + 3x - 1$ 12) $5x^8 - 2x^6 - 10x^4 + 4x^2$

Composition of Functions

1) -13
2) -1
3) 26
4) -10
5) -17
6) 10
7) $\frac{25}{8}$
8) $\frac{1}{8}$
9) 8
10) $\frac{5}{8}$
11) $\frac{49}{8}$
12) $-\frac{1}{2}(x^2 - \frac{3}{2})$
13) 1
14) -2
15) 2
16) 6
17) -1
18) $-2x$
19) 3
20) -9
21) 2
22) $\sqrt{13}$
23) -7
24) -18

Quadratic Equations

1) $x^2 + 2x - 24$
2) $x^2 + 12x + 35$
3) $x^2 + 2x - 48$
4) $x^2 - 7x - 18$
5) $x^2 - 15x + 56$
6) $3x^2 - 7x - 6$
7) $4x^2 + 5x - 6$
8) $4x^2 - x - 5$
9) $7x^2 - 41x - 6$
10) $15x^2 - 12x - 3$
11) $(x-4)(x+2)$
12) $(x+5)(x+3)$
13) $(x-6)(x+4)$
14) $(x-3)(x-7)$
15) $(x+3)(x+7)$
16) $(4x+5)(x+1)$
17) $(5x-2)(x+3)$
18) $(5x-3)(x+4)$
19) $(2x+5)(x+1)$
20) $3(x-2)(3x-1)$
21) $x=-6, x=3$
22) $x=-1, x=-8$
23) $x=-2, x=-5$
24) $x=1, x=-2$
25) $x=3, x=-4$
26) $x=-3, x=-8$
27) $x=-4, x=-\frac{1}{2}$
28) $x=4, x=-7$
29) $x=3, x=-4$
30) $x=-3, x=2$

Solving quadratic equations

1) $\{-9, 1\}$
2) $\{-6, -7\}$
3) $\{8, -3\}$
4) $\{6, 4\}$
5) $\{-2, -12\}$
6) $\{-\frac{4}{5}, -7\}$
7) $\{-\frac{5}{4}, -\frac{1}{6}\}$
8) $\{-\frac{7}{2}, -8\}$
9) $\{-6, -5\}$
10) $\{-\frac{1}{6}, -8\}$
11) $\{8, 0\}$
12) $\{4, -4\}$
13) $\{2, 1\}$
14) $\{-4, -1\}$
15) $\{1, -9\}$
16) $\{2, -12\}$
17) $\{2, -8\}$
18) $\{-3, -6\}$
19) $\{-4, -9\}$
20) $\{5, -3\}$
21) $\{-5, -3\}$
22) $\{1, 3\}$
23) $\{\frac{6}{5}, \frac{3}{2}\}$
24) $\{\frac{6}{7}, 0\}$
25) $\{-\frac{7}{2}, 2\}$
26) $\{\frac{3}{5}, 2\}$
27) $\{-\frac{4}{3}, -4\}$
28) $\{-8, -7\}$
29) $\{4, -1\}$
30) $\{3, -6\}$
31) $\{3, 8\}$
32) $\{\frac{15}{17}, 0\}$

WWW.MathNotion.Com

Algebra 2

Quadratic formula and the discriminant

1) 576
2) 68
3) 8
4) −11
5) 28
6) 116
7) −11
8) 52
9) 40
10) 69
11) 64
12) 169
13) 336
14) 33
15) 316
16) 132
17) 104
18) 16
19) 1
20) 33

21) 0, one real solution
22) 0, one real solution
23) −783, no solution
24) 0, one real solution
25) −127, no solution
26) 0, one real solution
27) −703, no solution
28) 0, one real solution

Graphing quadratic functions

1) $(-3, 2), x = -3$

2) $(3, -2), x = 3$

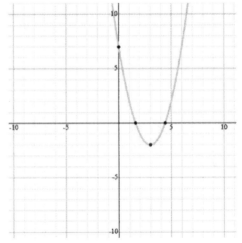

3) $(4, 6), x = 4$

4) $(-1, 12), x = -1$

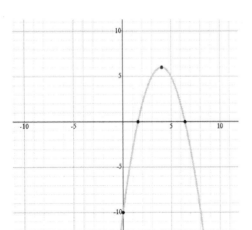
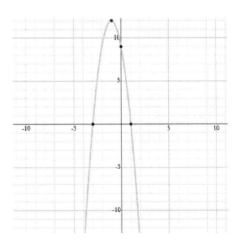

Algebra 2

Quadratic inequalities

1) $-5 < x < 5$
2) $-4 < x < -2$
3) no solution
4) $x < -4 \text{ or } x > -4$
5) $x \le -1 \text{ or } x \ge 10$
6) $x < -5 \text{ or } x > -5$
7) no solution
8) $-2 \le x \le 7$
9) $x \le -1 \text{ or } x \ge 7$
10) $-9 < x < 1$
11) $x < -12 \text{ or } x > 6$
12) $-3 < x < 4$
13) no solution
14) $x = 6$
15) $x \le 7 \text{ or } x \ge 9$
16) $x \le 5 \text{ or } x \ge 11$
17) $-9 \le x \le 9$
18) $x \le 3 \text{ or } x \ge 14$
19) no solution
20) $x < -3 \text{ or } x > 4$
21) no solution
22) $x \le 1 \text{ or } x \ge 5$
23) $x < -3 \text{ or } x > 5$
24) $x \ge 3$
25) $x < -6 \text{ or } x > 3$
26) $-6 < x < 1$
27) no solution
28) $x \le -1 \text{ or } x \ge 6$
29) $-5 < x < -3$
30) no solution
31) $x \le -4 \text{ or } x \ge 3$
32) $x \le -1 \text{ or } x \ge 3$

Domain and range of radical functions

1) domain: $x \ge -8$
   range: $y \ge -7$
2) domain: {all real numbers}
   range: {all real numbers}
3) domain: $x \ge 3$
   range: $y \ge 3$
4) domain: {all real numbers}
   range: {all real numbers}
5) domain: $x \ge -5$
   range: $y \ge 6$
6) domain: {all real numbers}
   range: {all real numbers}
7) domain: {all real numbers}
   range: $y \ge 8\sqrt{2} + 3$
8) domain: {all real numbers}
   range: {all real numbers}
9) domain: $x \ge -2$
   range: $y \ge -3$
10) domain: {all real numbers}
    range: {all real numbers}
11) domain: $x \le -2$
    range: $y \ge 5$
12) domain: {all real numbers}
    range: {all real numbers}
13) domain: $x \ge 5$
    range: $y \ge -2$
14) domain: {all real numbers}
    range: {all real numbers}

Algebra 2

15)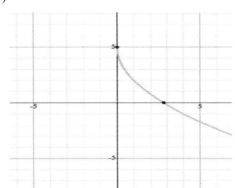

16)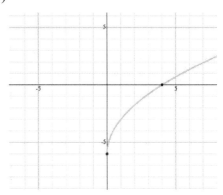

Solving radical equations

1) {81}
2) {36}
3) {16}
4) {$\frac{1}{4}$}
5) {321}
6) {43}
7) {19}
8) {54}
9) {148}
10) {59}

11) {5}
12) {32}
13) {6}
14) {72}
15) {194}
16) {0}
17) {20}
18) {5}
19) {2}
20) {9}

21) {2}
22) no solution
23) {−2}
24) {7}
25) {6}
26) {0}
27) {−4}
28) {−1}
29) {17}
30) {40}

Algebra 2

Chapter 5:
Monomials and Polynomials

Topics that you'll practice in this chapter:

- ✓ GCF of Monomials
- ✓ Factoring Quadratics
- ✓ Factoring by Grouping
- ✓ GCF and Powers of Monomials
- ✓ Writing Polynomials in Standard Form
- ✓ Simplifying Polynomials
- ✓ Adding and Subtracting Polynomials
- ✓ Multiplying Monomials
- ✓ Multiplying and Dividing Monomials
- ✓ Multiplying a Polynomial and a Monomial
- ✓ Multiplying Binomials
- ✓ Factoring Trinomials
- ✓ Operations with Polynomials

Mathematics is, as it were, a sensuous logic, and relates to philosophy as do the arts, music, and plastic art to poetry. — *K. Shegel*

Algebra 2

GCF of Monomials

✏ Find the GCF of each set of monomials.

1) $26xy, 14x$

2) $40a, 16a^2$

3) $15x^3, 45x^3$

4) $48x^4, 36x^6$

5) $10a^2, 40a^2b$

6) $70a^2, 20a^2b$

7) $32x^2, 24x^2$

8) $55x, 77y^4x$

9) $18, 24x^2, 36$

10) $15v^2, 60v, 45v$

11) p^3q^3, pqn

12) $12m^3n, 18m^3n^3$

13) $15x^3y, 5xy^3z$

14) $44m^2n^3, 66m^4n^5$

15) $28x^4y, 21x^3$

16) $18ab^6, 8a^3b^3c$

17) $25t^2u^3, 35t^4u^2$

18) $16t, 64t^2$

19) $14r^5q, 28pr^3t^2$

20) $20ab^4, 60a^3b$

21) $12d, 42ab^3$

22) $16a^2b^2, 24bc$

23) $10db, 35db$

24) $21m^2n^3, 42m^3n^2$

25) $8xyz, 4x^2$

26) $6x^2yz^{10}, 2x^2yz^4$

27) $120xz, 120y^3, 30y^3$

28) $32b, 40b, 32cb^2$

29) $20x^4, 15x^4, 25x$

30) $110b, 80bc, 70b$

WWW.MathNotion.Com

Algebra 2

Factoring Quadratics

✏ **Factor each completely.**

1) $x^2 - 13x + 40 =$

2) $m^2 - 11m + 18 =$

3) $p^2 + 2p - 48 =$

4) $3b^2 + 29b + 40 =$

5) $a^2 - 4a + 3 =$

6) $a^2 - 7a + 10 =$

7) $5n^2 - 28n + 32 =$

8) $t^2 - 11t + 28 =$

9) $4x^3 - 27x^2 + 18x =$

10) $x^2 - 10x + 21 =$

11) $7r^2 - 37r + 36 =$

12) $4n^2 b - 37nb + 40b =$

13) $3x^2 - 44x + 96 =$

14) $b^3 - 12b^2 + 27b =$

15) $5m^2 - 48m + 27 =$

16) $2x^3 - 23x^2 + 56x =$

17) $x^2 - 13x + 42 =$

18) $p^2 - 13p + 12 =$

19) $x^2 - 14x + 24 =$

20) $8x^2 - 59x + 21 =$

21) $12n^2 - 7n - 10 =$

22) $-3x^2 - 28x - 49 =$

23) $-8x^2 - 2x + 3 =$

24) $6x^2 + 13x - 63 =$

25) $12x^2 - 68x + 40 =$

26) $7x^2 - 48x + 36 =$

27) $8n^2 + 76n + 96 =$

28) $5x^2 - 18x + 9 =$

29) $5x^2 - 35xy =$

30) $-10x^3 - 124x^2 y - 48y^2 x =$

31) $16a^2 + 8ab - 15b^2 =$

32) $25x^2 - 10xy - 8y^2 =$

33) $64x^2 y - 152xy^2 + 90y^3 =$

34) $3x^2 - 12xy - 63y^2 =$

35) $56mp^2 - 49mp =$

36) $27b^2 + 150b + 75 =$

37) $12x^2 + 90xy + 162y^2 =$

38) $16x^2 + 14xy =$

WWW.MathNotion.Com

Algebra 2

Factoring by Grouping

✎ **Factor each completely.**

1) $18xy - 24x + 3ky - 4k =$

2) $12xy - 10x + 6ny - 5n =$

3) $15n^3 + 10n^2 + 6n + 4 =$

4) $9u^2v + 36u^4 - 6umv - 24u^3m =$

5) $24n^4 + 8n^3 + 36n^2 + 12n =$

6) $16uv - 8u^2 + 24bv - 12bu =$

7) $2x^3 + 6x^2 + 9x + 27 =$

8) $4x^3 + 16x^2 + 8x + 32 =$

9) $3m^3 - 3m^2 + 6m - 6 =$

10) $3x^3 - 9x^2 - 18x + 54 =$

11) $6p^3 + 8p^2 - 15p - 20 =$

12) $18mc + 8md - 9n^2c - 4n^2d =$

13) $16x^4 + 32x^2 - 40x^2 - 80x =$

14) $8xw + 10kx + 12yw + 15ky =$

15) $25xy - 10x + 15ry - 6r =$

16) $3xy - 6x - 7y + 14 =$

17) $5x^3 - 40x^2 + 2x - 16 =$

18) $18x^3 - 126x^2 + 3x - 21 =$

19) $6x^3 + 21x^2 + 10x + 35 =$

20) $12x^3 + 36x^2 - 30x - 90 =$

WWW.MathNotion.Com

Algebra 2

GCF and Powers of Monomials

✏️ **Find the GCF of each pairs of expressions.**

1) $45x^4, 18x^4$

2) $66y, 88y^2x$

3) $18x^2, 24, 36$

4) $20a^3, 55a^2, 15a$

5) xp^3q^3, pq

6) $10m^2n, 45m^2n^2$

7) $15yz, 5xy^2$

8) $24m^8n^3, 16m^2n^2$

9) $18x^4, 27x^2y$

10) $12cb^5, 6a^2b^2c$

11) $15t^2u^6, 20t^4u^7$

12) $17t, 51t^6$

13) $19r^2tq, 38r^4t^9$

14) $12a^2b^9, 36a^8b^5$

15) $14f, 25ab^3$

16) $15a^3b^3c^2, 22abc$

17) $10ab, 5ab$

18) $32m^6n^2, 16m^3n^4$

19) $6xy, 3x^2$

20) $x^2yz^3, 3x^2yz^3$

✏️ **Simplify.**

21) $(2x^5)^3$

22) $(2y^3 3y^2y)^3$

23) $(4x^3 3x^3)^2$

24) $(5x^2y^4)^4$

25) $(2y^2 2y^3)^5$

26) $(3x^2y)^7$

27) $(5x^3x^3 2n)^3$

28) $(4xy^4)^6$

29) $(8x^4y^2)^3$

30) $(14y^5y^2)^2$

31) $(5x^3x^4)^4$

32) $(2x^8 6x^2k^3)^2$

33) $(y^6 3y^2)^3$

34) $(2x 2x^4)^7$

35) $(8y^6)^2$

36) $(2y^2 y^5 y^2)^4$

37) $(6y^3y)^4$

38) $(5xy^5)^4$

WWW.MathNotion.Com

Algebra 2

Writing Polynomials in Standard Form

✏️ **Write each polynomial in standard form.**

1) $11x - 7x =$

2) $-5 + 19x - 19x =$

3) $6x^5 - 12x^3 =$

4) $12 + 17x^4 - 12 =$

5) $5x^2 + 4x - 9x^3 =$

6) $-3x^2 + 12x^5 =$

7) $5x + 8x^3 - 2x^8 =$

8) $-7x^3 + 4x - 9x^6 =$

9) $3x^2 + 22 - 6x =$

10) $3 - 4x + 9x^4 =$

11) $13x^2 + 28x - 8x^3 =$

12) $16 + 4x^2 - 2x^3 =$

13) $19x^2 - 9x + 9x^4 =$

14) $3x^4 - 7x^2 - 2x^3 =$

15) $-51 + 3x^2 - 8x^4 =$

16) $7x^2 - 8x^6 + 4x^4 - 15 =$

17) $6x^4 - 4x^5 + 16 - 3x^3 =$

18) $-2x^6 + 4x - 7x^2 - 5x =$

19) $11x^7 + 8x^5 - 5x^7 - 3x^2 =$

20) $2x^2 - 12x^5 + 8x^2 + 3x^6 =$

21) $4x^5 - 11x^7 - 6x^3 + 16x^5 =$

22) $6x^3 + 3x^5 + 34x^4 - 8x^5 =$

23) $3x(4x + 5 - 2x^2) =$

24) $12x(x^6 + 4x^3) =$

25) $5x(3x^2 + 6x + 4) =$

26) $7x(4 - 2x + 6x^5) =$

27) $3x(4x^4 - 4x^3 + 2) =$

28) $4x(2x^5 + 6x^2 - 3) =$

29) $5x(3x^4 + 4x^3 + 2x) =$

30) $2x(3x - 2x^3 + 4x^6) =$

WWW.MathNotion.Com

Algebra 2

Simplifying Polynomials

✎ **Simplify each expression.**

1) $3(4x - 20) =$

2) $5x(3x - 4) =$

3) $6x(5x - 7) =$

4) $3x(7x + 5) =$

5) $5x(4x - 3) =$

6) $6x(8x + 2) =$

7) $(3x - 2)(x - 4) =$

8) $(x - 5)(2x + 6) =$

9) $(x - 3)(x - 7) =$

10) $(3x + 4)(3x - 4) =$

11) $(5x - 4)(5x - 2) =$

12) $6x^2 + 6x^2 - 8x^4 =$

13) $3x - 2x^2 + 5x^3 + 7 =$

14) $7x + 4x^2 - 10x^3 =$

15) $12x^2 + 5x^5 - 6x^3 =$

16) $-5x^2 + 4x^6 + 6x^8 =$

17) $-12x^3 + 10x^5 - 4x^6 + 4x =$

18) $11 - 7x^2 + 4x^2 - 16x^3 + 11 =$

19) $2x^2 - 9x + 4x^3 + 15x - 10x =$

20) $13 - 7x^5 + 6x^5 - 4x^2 + 5 =$

21) $-5x^8 + x^6 - 14x^3 + 5x^8 =$

22) $(7x^4 - 4) + (7x^4 - 2x^4) =$

23) $3(3x^4 - 4x^3 - 6x^4) =$

24) $-5(x^9 + 8) - 5(10 - x^9) =$

25) $8x^3 - 9x^4 - 2x + 19 - 8x^3 =$

26) $11 - 8x^3 + 6x^3 - 7x^5 + 6 =$

27) $(5x^3 - 4x) - (6x - 2 - 6x^3) =$

28) $4x^2 - 5x^4 - x(3x^3 + 2x) =$

29) $6x + 6x^5 - 10 - 4(x^5 - 3) =$

30) $4 - 3x^4 + (6x^5 - 2x^4 + 5x^5) =$

31) $-(x^5 + 4) - 8(3 + x^5) =$

32) $(4x^3 - 3x) - (3x - 5x^3) =$

WWW.MathNotion.Com

Algebra 2

Adding and Subtracting Polynomials

✎ **Add or subtract expressions.**

1) $(-2x^2 - 3) + (3x^2 + 4) =$

2) $(4x^3 + 6) - (7 - 2x^3) =$

3) $(4x^5 + 5x^2) - (2x^5 + 15) =$

4) $(6x^3 - 2x^2) + (5x^2 - 4x) =$

5) $(10x^4 + 28x) - (34x^4 + 6) =$

6) $(7x^2 - 3) + (7x^2 + 3) =$

7) $(9x^2 + 4) - (10 - 5x^2) =$

8) $(6x^2 + x^5) - (x^5 + 4) =$

9) $(4x^3 - x) + (3x - 7x^3) =$

10) $(11x + 10) - (8x + 10) =$

11) $(15x^3 - 3x) - (3x - 4x^3) =$

12) $(4x - x^5) - (6x^5 + 8x) =$

13) $(2x^2 - 7x^7) - (4x^7 - 6x) =$

14) $(3x^2 - 5) + (8x^2 + 4x^5) =$

15) $(9x^4 + 5x^5) - (x^5 - 9x^4) =$

16) $(-4x^3 - 2x) + (9x - 5x^3) =$

17) $(4x - 3x^2) - (148x^2 + x) =$

18) $(5x - 8x^4) - (3x^4 - 4x^2) =$

19) $(8x^4 - 4) + (2x^4 - 3x^2) =$

20) $(5x^6 + 7x^3) - (x^3 - 5x^6) =$

21) $(-2x^2 + 20x^5 + 5x^4) + (12x^4 + 8x^5 + 24x^2) =$

22) $(7x^4 - 9x^7 - 6x) - (-3x^4 - 9x^7 + 6x) =$

23) $(14x + 12x^4 - 18x^6) + (20x^4 + 18x^6 - 10x) =$

24) $(5x^8 - 6x^6 - 4x) - (5x^3 + 9x^6 - 7x) =$

25) $(11x^2 - 6x^4 - 3x) - (-4x^2 - 12x^4 + 9x) =$

26) $(-5x^9 + 14x^3 + 3x^7) + (10x^7 + 26x^3 + 3x^9) =$

WWW.MathNotion.Com

Algebra 2

Multiplying Monomials

✎ **Simplify each expression.**

1) $6u^8 \times (-u^2) =$

2) $(-5p^8) \times (-2p^3) =$

3) $4xy^3z^5 \times 3z^4 =$

4) $3u^5t \times 8ut^4 =$

5) $(-5a^2) \times (-7a^3b^6) =$

6) $-3a^4b^3 \times 6a^2b =$

7) $13xy^5 \times x^4y^4 =$

8) $6p^4q^3 \times (-8pq^6) =$

9) $8s^4t^3 \times 4st^3 =$

10) $(-6x^4y^3) \times 6x^2y =$

11) $3xy^7z \times 12z^3 =$

12) $24xy \times x^2y =$

13) $13pq^4 \times (-3p^2q) =$

14) $13s^3t^4 \times st^4 =$

15) $11p^5 \times (-6p^3) =$

16) $(-8p^3q^5r) \times 3pq^4r^6 =$

17) $(-4a^4) \times (-7a^3b) =$

18) $6u^6v^2 \times (-5u^3v^4) =$

19) $9u^5 \times (-3u) =$

20) $-6xy^5 \times 4x^2y =$

21) $13y^5z^3 \times (-y^3z) =$

22) $8a^4bc^3 \times 2abc^3 =$

23) $(-7p^5q^6) \times (-5p^4q^2) =$

24) $4u^5v^3 \times (-4u^7v^3) =$

25) $17y^4z^5 \times (-y^6z) =$

26) $(-5pq^3r^2) \times 8p^2q^4r =$

27) $3ab^5c^6 \times 5a^4bc^2 =$

28) $6x^3yz^2 \times 3x^2y^7z^3 =$

WWW.MathNotion.Com

Algebra 2

Multiplying and Dividing Monomials

✏️ Simplify each expression.

1) $(5x^5)(2x^2) =$

2) $(4x^4)(6x^2) =$

3) $(3x^4)(7x^4) =$

4) $(5x^6)(4x^2) =$

5) $(12x^4)(3x^6) =$

6) $(4yx^8)(8y^4x^3) =$

7) $(14x^4y)(x^3y^5) =$

8) $(-5x^3y^4)(2x^3y^5) =$

9) $(-6x^4y^2)(-3x^3y^5) =$

10) $(5x^3y)(-5x^2y^3) =$

11) $(6x^4y^3)(4x^3y^4) =$

12) $(4x^3y^2)(5x^2y^4) =$

13) $(12x^3y^6)(4x^4y^{10}) =$

14) $(15x^3y^5)(3x^4y^6) =$

15) $(7x^2y^7)(8x^6y^7) =$

16) $(-3x^3y^8)(7x^9y^4) =$

17) $\dfrac{5x^6y^6}{xy^4} =$

18) $\dfrac{19x^7y^5}{19x^6y} =$

19) $\dfrac{56x^4y^4}{8xy} =$

20) $\dfrac{81x^5y^6}{9x^4y^5} =$

21) $\dfrac{36x^7y^6}{9x^2y^3} =$

22) $\dfrac{48x^9y^7}{4x^4y^6} =$

23) $\dfrac{88x^{18}y^{12}}{11x^8y^9} =$

24) $\dfrac{30x^7y^6}{6x^8y^3} =$

25) $\dfrac{150x^7y^6}{30x^4y^6} =$

26) $\dfrac{-42x^{18}y^{14}}{6x^4y^9} =$

27) $\dfrac{-36x^7y^8}{9x^5y^8} =$

WWW.MathNotion.Com

Algebra 2

Multiplying a Polynomial and a Monomial

✏️ **Find each product.**

1) $x(2x + 4) =$

2) $6(4 - 2x) =$

3) $5x(4x + 2) =$

4) $x(-4x + 5) =$

5) $8x(2x - 2) =$

6) $6(2x - 4y) =$

7) $7x(5x - 5) =$

8) $3x(12x + 2y) =$

9) $4x(x + 6y) =$

10) $11x(3x + 4y) =$

11) $7x(3x + 2) =$

12) $10x(4x - 10y) =$

13) $9x(3x - 2y) =$

14) $7x(x - 4y + 6) =$

15) $8x(2x^2 + 5y^2) =$

16) $12x(2x + 3y) =$

17) $4(2x^4 - 4y^4) =$

18) $4x(-3x^2y + 4y) =$

19) $-4(5x^3 - 2xy + 4) =$

20) $4(x^2 - 5xy - 6) =$

21) $8x(2x^3 - 5xy + 2x) =$

22) $-6x(-2x^3 - 6x + 2xy) =$

23) $3(2x^2 + xy - 9y^2) =$

24) $4x(5x^3 - 3x + 7) =$

25) $6(3x^{22} - 2x - 5) =$

26) $x^2(-2x^3 + 4x + 3) =$

27) $x^2(4x^3 + 10 - 2x) =$

28) $4x^4(3x^3 - 2x + 5) =$

29) $2x^2(4x^4 - 5xy + 7y^3) =$

30) $5x^2(5x^4 - 3x + 9) =$

31) $7x^2(6x^2 + 3x - 6) =$

32) $4x(x^3 - 4xy + 2y^2) =$

WWW.MathNotion.Com

Algebra 2

Multiplying Binomials

✏️ **Find each product.**

1) $(x + 3)(x + 6) =$

2) $(x - 4)(x + 3) =$

3) $(x - 3)(x - 8) =$

4) $(x + 8)(x + 9) =$

5) $(x - 2)(x - 12) =$

6) $(x + 5)(x + 5) =$

7) $(x - 6)(x + 7) =$

8) $(x - 8)(x - 3) =$

9) $(x + 7)(x + 12) =$

10) $(x - 4)(x + 8) =$

11) $(x + 8)(x + 8) =$

12) $(x + 2)(x + 7) =$

13) $(x - 6)(x + 6) =$

14) $(x - 5)(x + 5) =$

15) $(x + 11)(x + 11) =$

16) $(x + 6)(x + 9) =$

17) $(x - 2)(x + 2) =$

18) $(x - 4)(x + 7) =$

19) $(3x + 5)(x + 6) =$

20) $(5x - 6)(4x + 8) =$

21) $(x - 7)(3x + 7) =$

22) $(x - 9)(x - 4) =$

23) $(x - 12)(x + 2) =$

24) $(2x - 4)(5x + 4) =$

25) $(3x - 8)(x + 8) =$

26) $(7x - 2)(6x + 3) =$

27) $(4x + 5)(3x + 5) =$

28) $(7x - 4)(9x + 4) =$

29) $(x + 2)(2x - 8) =$

30) $(5x - 4)(5x + 4) =$

31) $(3x + 2)(3x - 7) =$

32) $(x^2 + 8)(x^2 - 8) =$

WWW.MathNotion.Com

Algebra 2

Factoring Trinomials

✎ **Factor each trinomial.**

1) $x^2 + 8x + 12 =$

2) $x^2 - 6x + 5 =$

3) $x^2 + 15x + 36 =$

4) $x^2 - 12x + 35 =$

5) $x^2 - 11x + 18 =$

6) $x^2 - 9x + 18 =$

7) $x^2 + 18x + 72 =$

8) $x^2 - x - 72 =$

9) $x^2 + 4x - 21 =$

10) $x^2 - 13x + 22 =$

11) $x^2 + 2x - 24 =$

12) $x^2 - 3x - 40 =$

13) $x^2 - 3x - 70 =$

14) $x^2 + 26x + 169 =$

15) $4x^2 - 7x - 15 =$

16) $x^2 - 14x + 33 =$

17) $10x^2 + 5x - 15 =$

18) $6x^2 - 4x - 42 =$

19) $x^2 + 12x + 36 =$

20) $5x^2 + 17x - 12 =$

✎ **Calculate each problem.**

21) The area of a rectangle is $x^2 - x - 56$. If the width of rectangle is $x + 7$, what is its length? _____

22) The area of a parallelogram is $4x^2 + 17x - 15$ and its height is $x + 5$. What is the base of the parallelogram? _____

23) The area of a rectangle is $6x^2 - 22x + 12$. If the width of the rectangle is $3x - 2$, what is its length? _____

Algebra 2

Operations with Polynomials

✎ **Find each product.**

1) $4(5x + 3) =$ _____

2) $8(2x + 6) =$ _____

3) $2(5x - 2) =$ _____

4) $-4(7x - 3) =$ _____

5) $3x^2(9x + 1) =$ _____

6) $4x^6(7x - 9) =$ _____

7) $3x^4(-7x + 3) =$ _____

8) $-8x^4(5x - 8) =$ _____

9) $7(x^2 + 5x - 3) =$ _____

10) $9(5x^2 - 7x + 5) =$ _____

11) $3(3x^2 + 3x + 2) =$ _____

12) $5x(3x^2 + 5x + 8) =$ _____

13) $(5x + 7)(3x - 3) =$ _____

14) $(9x + 3)(3x - 5) =$ _____

15) $(6x + 3)(4x - 2) =$ _____

16) $(7x - 2)(3x + 5) =$ _____

✎ **Calculate each problem.**

17) The measures of two sides of a triangle are $(2x + 5y)$ and $(6x - 3y)$. If the perimeter of the triangle is $(13x + 4y)$, what is the measure of the third side? _____

18) The height of a triangle is $(8x + 5)$ and its base is $(4x - 3)$. What is the area of the triangle? _____

19) One side of a square is $(6x + 2)$. What is the area of the square? _____

20) The length of a rectangle is $(5x - 8y)$ and its width is $(15x + 8y)$. What is the perimeter of the rectangle? _____

21) The side of a cube measures $(x + 2)$. What is the volume of the cube? _____

22) If the perimeter of a rectangle is $(28x + 6y)$ and its width is $(5x + 2y)$, what is the length of the rectangle? _____

WWW.MathNotion.Com

Algebra 2

Answers of Worksheets

GCF of Monomials

1) $2x$
2) $8a$
3) $15x^3$
4) $12x^4$
5) $10a^2$
6) $10a^2$
7) $8x^2$
8) $11x$
9) 6
10) $15v$
11) pq
12) $6m^3n$
13) $5xy$
14) $22m^2n^2$
15) $7x^3$
16) $2ab^3$
17) $5t^2u^2$
18) $16t$
19) $14r^3$
20) $20ab$
21) 6
22) $8b$
23) $5db$
24) $21m^2n^2$
25) $4x$
26) $2x^2yz^4$
27) 30
28) $8b$
29) $5x$
30) $10a$

Factoring Quadratics

1) $(x-5)(x-8)$
2) $(m-2)(m-9)$
3) $(p+8)(p-6)$
4) $(3b+5)(b+8)$
5) $(a-1)(a-3)$
6) $(a-2)(a-5)$
7) $(5n-8)(n-4)$
8) $(t-7)(t-4)$
9) $x(4x-3)(x-6)$
10) $(x-3)(x-7)$
11) $(7r-9)(r-4)$
12) $b(4n-5)(n-8)$
13) $(3x-8)(x-12)$
14) $b(b-3)(b-9)$
15) $(5m-3)(m-9)$
16) $x(2x-7)(x-8)$
17) $(x-6)(x-7)$
18) $(p-1)(p-12)$
19) $(x-2)(x-12)$
20) $(8x-3)(x-7)$
21) $(4n-5)(3n+2)$
22) $-(3x+7)(x+7)$
23) $-(4x+3)(2x-1)$
24) $(2x+9)(3x-7)$
25) $4(x-5)(3x-2)$
26) $(7x-6)(x-6)$
27) $4(2n+3)(n+8)$
28) $(5x-3)(x-3)$
29) $5x(x-7y)$
30) $-2x(5x+2y)(x+12y)$
31) $(4a+5b)(4a-3b)$
32) $(5x+2y)(5x-4y)$
33) $2y(8x-9y)(4x-5y)$
34) $3(x-7y)(x+3y)$
35) $7mp(8p-7)$
36) $3(9b+5)(b+5)$

Algebra 2

37) $6(2x + 9y)(x + 3y)$ 38) $2x(8x + 7y)$

Factoring by Grouping

1) $(6x + k)(3y - 4)$
2) $(2x + n)(6y - 5)$
3) $(5n^2 + 2)(3n + 2)$
4) $3u(3u - 2m)(v + 4u^2)$
5) $4n(2n^2 + 3)(3n + 1)$
6) $4(2u + 3b)(2v - u)$
7) $(2x^2 + 9)(x + 3)$
8) $4(x^2 + 2)(x + 4)$
9) $3(m^2 + 2)(m - 1)$
10) $3(x^2 - 6)(x - 3)$
11) $(2p^2 - 5)(3p + 4)$
12) $(2m - n^2)(9c + 4d)$
13) $8x(2x^2 - 5)(x + 2)$
14) $(2x + 3y)(4w + 5k)$
15) $(5x + 3r)(5y - 2)$
16) $(3x - 7)(y - 2)$
17) $(5x^2 + 2)(x - 8)$
18) $3(6x^2 + 1)(x - 7)$
19) $(3x^2 + 5)(2x + 7)$
20) $6(2x^2 - 5)(x + 3)$

GCF and Powers of monomials

1) $9x^4$
2) $22y$
3) 6
4) $5a$
5) pq
6) $5m^2n$
7) $5y$
8) $8m^2n^2$
9) $9x^2$
10) $6cb^2$
11) $5t^2u^6$
12) $17t$
13) $19r^2t$
14) $12a^2b^5$
15) 1
16) abc
17) $5ab$
18) $16m^3n^4$
19) $3x$
20) x^2yz^3
21) $8x^{15}$
22) $216y^{18}$
23) $144y^{12}$
24) $625x^8y^{16}$
25) $1,024y^{25}$
26) $2,187x^{14}y^7$
27) $1,000n^3x^{18}$
28) $4,096x^6y^{24}$
29) $512x^{12}y^6$
30) $196y^{14}$
31) $625x^{28}$
32) $144x^{20}k^6$
33) $27y^{24}$
34) $16,384x^{35}$
35) $64y^{12}$
36) $16x^{36}$
37) $1,296y^{36}$
38) $625x^4y^{20}$

Writing Polynomials in Standard Form

1) $4x$
2) -5
3) $6x^5 - 12x^3$
4) $14x^4$

Algebra 2

5) $-9x^3 + 5x^2 + 4x$

6) $12x^5 - 3x^2$

7) $-2x^8 + 8x^3 + 5x$

8) $-9x^6 - 7x^3 + 4x$

9) $3x^2 - 6x + 22$

10) $9x^4 - 4x + 3$

11) $-8x^3 + 13x^2 + 28x$

12) $-2x^3 + 4x^2 + 16$

13) $9x^4 + 19x^2 - 9x$

14) $3x^4 - 2x^3 - 7x^2$

15) $-8x^4 + 3x^2 - 51$

16) $-8x^6 + 4x^4 + 7x^2 - 15$

17) $-4x^5 + 6x^4 - 3x^3 + 16$

18) $-2x^6 - 7x^2 - x$

19) $6x^7 + 8x^5 - 3x^2$

20) $3x^6 - 12x^5 + 10x^2$

21) $-11x^7 + 20x^5 - 6x^3$

22) $-5x^5 + 34x^4 + 6x^3$

23) $-6x^3 + 12x^2 + 15x$

24) $12x^7 + 48x^4$

25) $15x^3 + 30x^2 + 20x$

26) $42x^6 - 14x^2 + 28x$

27) $12x^5 - 12x^4 + 6x$

28) $8x^6 + 24x^3 - 12x$

29) $15x^5 + 20x^4 + 10x^2$

30) $8x^7 - 4x^4 + 6x^2$

Simplifying Polynomials

1) $12x - 60$

2) $15x^2 - 20x$

3) $30x^2 - 42x$

4) $21x^2 + 15x$

5) $20x^2 - 15x$

6) $48x^2 + 12x$

7) $3x^2 - 14x + 8$

8) $2x^2 - 4x - 30$

9) $x^2 - 10x + 21$

10) $9x^2 - 16$

11) $25x^2 - 30x + 8$

12) $-8x^4 + 12x^2$

13) $5x^3 - 2x^2 + 3x + 7$

14) $-10x^3 + 4x^2 + 7x$

15) $5x^5 - 6x^3 + 12x^2$

16) $6x^8 + 4x^6 - 5x^2$

17) $-4x^6 + 10x^5 - 12x^3 + 4x$

18) $-16x^3 - 3x^2 + 22$

19) $4x^3 + 2x^2 - 4x$

20) $-x^5 - 4x^2 + 18$

21) $x^6 - 14x^3$

22) $12x^4 - 4$

23) $-9x^4 - 12x^3$

24) -90

25) $-9x^4 - 2x + 19$

26) $-7x^5 - 2x^3 + 17$

27) $11x^3 - 10x + 2$

28) $-8x^4 + 2x^2$

29) $2x^5 + 6x + 2$

30) $11x^5 - 5x^4 + 4$

31) $-9x^5 - 28$

32) $9x^3 - 6x$

Algebra 2

Adding and Subtracting Polynomials

1) $x^2 + 1$
2) $6x^3 - 1$
3) $2x^5 + 5x^2 - 15$
4) $6x^3 + 3x^2 - 4x$
5) $-24x^4 + 28x - 6$
6) $14x^2$
7) $14x^2 - 6$
8) $6x^2 - 4$
9) $-3x^3 + 2x$
10) $3x$
11) $19x^3 - 6x$
12) $-7x^5 - 4x$
13) $-11x^7 + 2x^2 + 6x$
14) $4x^5 + 11x^2 - 5$
15) $4x^5 + 18x^4$
16) $-9x^3 + 7x$
17) $-151x^2 + 3x$
18) $-11x^4 + 4x^2 + 5x$
19) $10x^4 - 3x^2 - 4$
20) $10x^6 + 6x^3$
21) $28x^5 + 17x^4 + 22x^2$
22) $10x^4 - 12x$
23) $32x^4 + 4x$
24) $5x^8 - 15x^6 - 5x^3 + 3x$
25) $6x^4 + 15x^2 - 12x$
26) $-2x^9 + 13x^7 + 40x^3$

Multiplying Monomials

1) $-6u^{10}$
2) $10p^{11}$
3) $12xy^3z^9$
4) $24u^6t^5$
5) $35a^5b^6$
6) $-18a^6b^4$
7) $13x^5y^9$
8) $-48p^5q^9$
9) $32s^5t^6$
10) $-36x^6y^4$
11) $36xy^7z^4$
12) $24px^3y^2$
13) $-39p^3q^5$
14) $13s^4t^8$
15) $-66p^8$
16) $-24p^4q^9r^7$
17) $28a^7b$
18) $-30u^9v^6$
19) $-27u^6$
20) $-24x^3y^6$
21) $-13y^8z^4$
22) $16a^5b^2c^6$
23) $35p^9q^8$
24) $-16u^{12}v^6$
25) $-17y^{10}z^6$
26) $-40p^3q^7r^3$
27) $15a^5b^6c^8$
28) $18x^5y^8z^5$

Multiplying and Dividing Monomials

1) $10x^7$
2) $24x^6$
3) $21x^8$
4) $20x^8$
5) $36x^{10}$
6) $32x^{11}y^5$
7) $14x^7y^6$
8) $-10x^6y^9$
9) $18x^7y^7$
10) $-25x^5y^4$
11) $24x^7y^7$
12) $20x^5y^6$
13) $48x^7y^{16}$
14) $45x^7y^{11}$
15) $56x^8y^{14}$
16) $-21x^{12}y^{12}$
17) $5x^5y^2$
18) xy^4
19) $7x^3y^3$
20) $9xy$
21) $4x^5y^3$
22) $12x^5y$
23) $8x^{10}y^3$
24) $5x^{-1}y^3$

Algebra 2

25) $5x^3$ 26) $-7x^{14}y^5$ 27) $-4x^2$

Multiplying a Polynomial and a Monomial

1) $2x^2 + 4x$
2) $-12x + 24$
3) $20x^2 + 10x$
4) $-4x^2 + 5x$
5) $16x^2 - 16x$
6) $12x - 24y$
7) $35x^2 - 35x$
8) $36x^2 + 6xy$
9) $4x^2 + 24xy$
10) $33x^2 + 44xy$
11) $21x^2 + 14x$
12) $40x^2 - 100xy$
13) $27x^2 - 18xy$
14) $7x^2 - 28xy + 42x$
15) $16x^3 + 40xy^2$
16) $24x^2 + 36xy$

17) $8x^4 - 16y^4$
18) $-12x^3y + 16xy$
19) $-20x^3 + 8xy - 16$
20) $4x^2 - 20xy - 24$
21) $16x^4 - 40x^2y + 16x^2$
22) $12x^4 + 36x^2 - 12x^2y$
23) $6x^2 + 3xy - 27y^2$
24) $20x^4 - 12x^2 + 28x$
25) $18x^{22} - 12x - 30$
26) $-2x^5 + 4x^3 + 3x^2$
27) $4x^5 - 2x^3 + 10x^2$
28) $12x^7 - 8x^5 + 20x^4$
29) $8x^6 - 10x^3y + 14x^2y^3$
30) $25x^6 - 15x^3 + 45x^2$
31) $42x^4 + 21x^3 - 42x^2$
32) $4x^4 - 16x^2y + 8xy^2$

Multiplying Binomials

1) $x^2 + 9x + 18$
2) $x^2 - x - 12$
3) $x^2 - 11x + 24$
4) $x^2 + 17x + 72$
5) $x^2 - 14x + 24$
6) $x^2 + 10x + 25$
7) $x^2 + x - 42$
8) $x^2 - 11x + 24$
9) $x^2 + 19x + 84$
10) $x^2 + 4x - 32$
11) $x^2 + 16x + 64$

12) $x^2 + 9x + 14$
13) $x^2 - 36$
14) $x^2 - 25$
15) $x^2 + 22x + 121$
16) $x^2 + 15x + 54$
17) $x^2 - 4$
18) $x^2 + 3x - 28$
19) $3x^2 + 23x + 30$
20) $20x^2 + 16x - 48$
21) $3x^2 - 14x - 49$
22) $x^2 - 13x + 36$

Algebra 2

23) $x^2 - 10x - 24$
24) $10x^2 - 12x - 16$
25) $3x^2 + 16x - 64$
26) $42x^2 + 9x - 6$
27) $12x^2 + 35x + 25$

28) $63x^2 - 8x - 16$
29) $2x^2 - 4x - 16$
30) $25x^2 - 16$
31) $9x^2 - 15x - 14$
32) $x^4 - 64$

Factoring Trinomials

1) $(x + 6)(x + 2)$
2) $(x - 5)(x - 1)$
3) $(x + 12)(x + 3)$
4) $(x - 5)(x - 7)$
5) $(x - 2)(x - 9)$
6) $(x - 6)(x - 3)$
7) $(x + 6)(x + 12)$
8) $(x + 8)(x - 9)$

9) $(x - 3)(x + 7)$
10) $(x - 11)(x - 2)$
11) $(x - 4)(x + 6)$
12) $(x - 8)(x + 5)$
13) $(x + 7)(x - 10)$
14) $(x + 13)(x + 13)$
15) $(4x + 5)(x - 3)$
16) $(x - 11)(x - 3)$

17) $(5x - 5)(2x + 3)$
18) $(2x - 6)(3x + 7)$
19) $(x + 6)(x + 6)$
20) $(5x - 3)(x + 4)$
21) $(x - 8)$
22) $(4x - 3)$
23) $(2x - 6)$

Operations with Polynomials

1) $20x + 12$
2) $16x + 48$
3) $10x - 4$
4) $-28x + 12$
5) $27x^3 + 3x^2$
6) $28x^7 - 36x^6$
7) $-21x^5 + 9x^4$
8) $-40x^5 + 64x^4$

9) $7x^2 + 35x - 21$
10) $45x^2 - 63x + 45$
11) $9x^2 + 9x + 6$
12) $15x^3 + 25x^2 + 40x$
13) $15x^2 + 6x - 21$
14) $27x^2 - 36x - 15$
15) $24x^2 - 6$
16) $21x^2 + 29x - 10$

17) $(5x + 2y)$
18) $16x^2 - 2x - \frac{15}{2}$
19) $36x^2 + 24x + 4$
20) $40x$
21) $x^3 + 6x^2 + 12x + 8$
22) $(9x + y)$

Algebra 2

Chapter 6 :
Complex Numbers

Topics that you'll practice in this chapter:

- ✓ Adding and Subtracting Complex Numbers
- ✓ Multiplying and Dividing Complex Numbers
- ✓ Graphing Complex Numbers
- ✓ Rationalizing Imaginary Denominators

Mathematics is a hard thing to love. It has the unfortunate habit, like a rude dog, of turning its most unfavorable side towards you when you first make contact with it. — David Whiteland

Algebra 2

Adding and Subtracting Complex Numbers

✎ **Simplify.**

1) $(7i) - (3i) =$ 4i

2) $(5i) + (4i) =$ 9i

3) $(2i) + (8i) =$ 10i

4) $(-8i) - (3i) =$ -5i

5) $(14i) + (6i) =$ 20i

6) $(6i) - (-10i) =$ -4i

7) $(-2i) + (-5i) =$ -7i

8) $(13i) - (5i) =$ 8i

9) $(-22i) - (11i) =$ -11i

10) $(-4i) + (2 + 6i) =$ 2+2i

11) $(10 - 5i) + (-3i) =$ 10-8i

12) $(-8i) + (6 + 12i) =$ 6+4i

13) $1 + (5 - 4i) =$ 6-4i

14) $(13i) - (-8 + 2i) =$ -8+11i

15) $(8 + 12i) - (-10i) =$ 9+2i

16) $(10 + i) + (-5i) =$ 10-4i

17) $(11i) - (-7i + 9) =$ 18i-9

18) $(10i + 12) + (-2i) =$

19) $(20) - (16 + 4i) =$

20) $(3 + 3i) + (8 + 4i) =$ 7i+11

21) $(15 - 7i) + (3 + 4i) =$ 18-3i

22) $(12 + 6i) + (10 + 17i) =$

23) $(-5 + 6i) - (-16 - 12i) =$

24) $(-4 + 14i) - (-9 + 11i) =$

25) $(-22 + 4i) - (-7 - 22i) =$

26) $(-26 - 18i) + (3 + 34i) =$

27) $(-19 - 13i) - (-7 - 20i) =$

28) $-21 + (5i) + (-32 + 14i) =$

29) $30 - (7i) + (3 - 11i) =$

30) $28 + (-32 - 10i) - 7 =$

31) $(-44i) + (2 - 7i) + 9 =$

32) $(-21i) - (12 - 9i) + 21i =$

WWW.MathNotion.Com

Algebra 2

Multiplying and Dividing Complex Numbers

✎ **Simplify.**

1) $(5i)(-3i) =$

2) $(-8i)(2i) =$

3) $(3i)(-3i)(-3i) =$

4) $(6i)(-6i) =$

5) $(-3 - 4i)(2 + i) =$

6) $(5 - 2i)^2 =$

7) $(5 - 2i)(6 - 4i) =$

8) $(1 + 6i)^2 =$

9) $(5i)(-3i)(2 - 4i) =$

10) $(11 - 2i)(2 - 4i) =$

11) $(-3 + i)(6 + 5i) =$

12) $(2 - 8i)(6 - 4i) =$

13) $3(4i) - (6i)(-2 + 5i) =$

14) $\dfrac{5}{-25i} =$

15) $\dfrac{3-4i}{-5i} =$

16) $\dfrac{6+12i}{2i} =$

17) $\dfrac{20i}{-5+4i} =$

18) $\dfrac{-6-9i}{4i} =$

19) $\dfrac{4i}{8-2i} =$

20) $\dfrac{4-7i}{6-2i} =$

21) $\dfrac{3-2i}{-1-1i} =$

22) $\dfrac{-5-5i}{-4-i} =$

23) $\dfrac{-6+2i}{-10-4i} =$

24) $\dfrac{-8-4i}{-2+4i} =$

25) $\dfrac{2+3i}{1-4i} =$

WWW.MathNotion.Com

Algebra 2

Graphing Complex Numbers

✎ Identify each complex number graphed.

1)

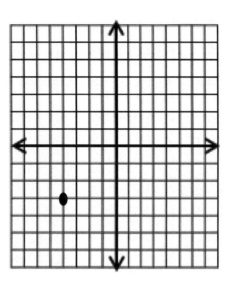

2)

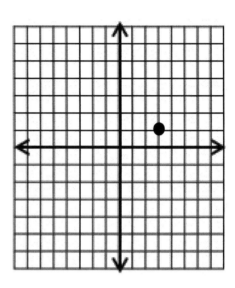

3)

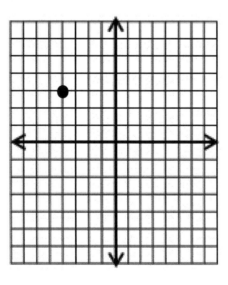

4)

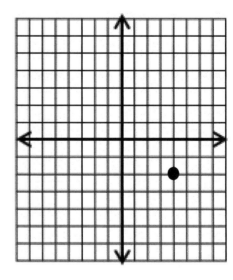

WWW.MathNotion.Com

Algebra 2

Rationalizing Imaginary Denominators

✎ **Simplify.**

1) $\dfrac{-7}{-7i} =$

2) $\dfrac{-3}{-15i} =$

3) $\dfrac{-3}{-39i} =$

4) $\dfrac{24}{-3i} =$

5) $\dfrac{5}{2i} =$

6) $\dfrac{16}{-4i} =$

7) $\dfrac{14}{-6i} =$

8) $\dfrac{-17}{3i} =$

9) $\dfrac{4x}{5yi} =$

10) $\dfrac{10-10i}{-2i} =$

11) $\dfrac{5-11i}{-i} =$

12) $\dfrac{21+4i}{4i} =$

13) $\dfrac{8i}{-1+4i} =$

14) $\dfrac{10i}{-6+8i} =$

15) $\dfrac{-25-5i}{-5+5i} =$

16) $\dfrac{-7-2i}{3+1i} =$

17) $\dfrac{-12-6i}{8-6i} =$

18) $\dfrac{-14+7i}{-7i} =$

19) $\dfrac{12+3i}{3i} =$

20) $\dfrac{-2-i}{4-3i} =$

21) $\dfrac{-11+4i}{-5i} =$

22) $\dfrac{8+2i}{-5-2i} =$

23) $\dfrac{-9-5i}{-8-2i} =$

24) $\dfrac{4i-1}{-5-2i} =$

WWW.MathNotion.Com

Algebra 2

Answers of Worksheets

Adding and Subtracting Complex Numbers

1) $4i$
2) $9i$
3) $10i$
4) $-11i$
5) $20i$
6) $16i$
7) $-7i$
8) $8i$
9) $-33i$
10) $2 + 2i$
11) $10 - 8i$
12) $6 + 4i$
13) $6 - 4i$
14) $8 + 11i$
15) $8 + 22i$
16) $10 - 4i$
17) $-9 + 18i$
18) $12 + 8i$
19) $4 - 4i$
20) $11 + 7i$
21) $18 - 3i$
22) $22 + 23i$
23) $11 + 18i$
24) $5 + 3i$
25) $-15 + 26i$
26) $-23 + 16i$
27) $-12 + 7i$
28) $-53 + 19i$
29) $33 - 18i$
30) $-11 - 10i$
31) $11 - 51i$
32) $-12 + 9i$

Multiplying and Dividing Complex Numbers

1) 15
2) 16
3) $-27i$
4) 36
5) $-2 - 11i$
6) $21 - 20i$
7) $22 - 32i$
8) $-35 + 12i$
9) $30 - 60i$
10) $14 - 48i$
11) $-23 - 9i$
12) $-20 - 56i$
13) $30 + 24i$
14) $\frac{i}{5}$
15) $\frac{4}{5} + \frac{3}{5}i$
16) $-6 + 3i$
17) $\frac{80}{41} - \frac{100}{41}i$
18) $\frac{9}{4} - \frac{3}{2}i$
19) $-\frac{2}{17} + \frac{8}{17}i$
20) $\frac{19}{20} - \frac{17}{20}i$
21) $-\frac{1}{2} + \frac{5}{2}i$
22) $\frac{25}{17} + \frac{15}{17}i$
23) $\frac{13}{29} - \frac{11}{29}i$
24) $2i$
25) $-\frac{10}{17} + \frac{11}{17}i$

Graphing Complex Numbers

1) $-4 - 3i$
2) $3 + i$
3) $-4 + 3i$
4) $4 - 2i$

Rationalizing Imaginary Denominators

1) $-i$
2) $-\frac{1}{5}i$
3) $\frac{-1}{13}i$
4) $8i$
5) $-\frac{5}{2}i$
6) $4i$
7) $\frac{7}{3}i$
8) $\frac{17}{3}i$
9) $-\frac{4x}{5y}i$
10) $5 + 5i$
11) $11 + 5i$
12) $1 - \frac{21}{4}i$
13) $\frac{32}{17} - \frac{8}{17}i$
14) $\frac{4}{5} - \frac{3}{5}i$
15) $2 + 3i$
16) $-\frac{23}{10} + \frac{1}{10}i$
17) $-\frac{3}{5} - \frac{6}{5}i$
18) $-1 - 2i$
19) $1 - 4i$
20) $-\frac{1}{5} - \frac{2}{5}i$
21) $-\frac{4}{5} - \frac{11}{5}i$
22) $-\frac{44}{29} + \frac{6}{29}i$
23) $\frac{41}{34} + \frac{11}{34}i$
24) $-\frac{3}{29} - \frac{22}{29}i$

Algebra 2

Chapter 7 :

Sequences and Series

Topics that you'll practice in this chapter:

- ✓ Arithmetic Sequences
- ✓ Geometric Sequences
- ✓ Comparing Arithmetic and Geometric Sequences
- ✓ Finite Geometric Series
- ✓ Infinite Geometric Series

Mathematics is like checkers in being suitable for the young, not too difficult, amusing, and without peril to the state. — Plato

Algebra 2

Arithmetic Sequences

✎ **Find the next three terms of each arithmetic sequence.**

1) 32, 26, 20, 14, 8, ...

2) −56, −44, −32, −20, ...

3) 17, 26, 35, 44, 53, ...

4) 5, 11, 17, 23, 29, ...

✎ **Given the first term and the common difference of an arithmetic sequence find the first five terms and the explicit formula.**

5) $a_1 = 20, d = 3$

6) $a_1 = -11, d = -5$

7) $a_1 = 32, d = 6$

8) $a_1 = 240, d = -80$

✎ **Given a term in an arithmetic sequence and the common difference find the first five terms and the explicit formula.**

9) $a_{20} = -500, d = -50$

10) $a_{24} = 98, d = 7$

11) $a_{51} = -88.2, d = -5.2$

12) $a_{68} = -980, d = -27$

✎ **Given a term in an arithmetic sequence and the common difference find the recursive formula and the three terms in the sequence after the last one given.**

13) $a_{21} = -187, d = -9$

14) $a_{12} = 63.5, d = 5.2$

15) $a_{31} = 58.2, d = 1.8$

16) $a_{42} = 6.8, d = 0.4$

WWW.MathNotion.Com

Algebra 2

Geometric Sequences

✎ **Determine if the sequence is geometric. If it is, find the common ratio.**

1) $1, -7, 49, -343, \ldots$

2) $-3, -12, -48, -192, \ldots$

3) $8, 24, 48, 240, \ldots$

4) $-5, -10, -20, -40, \ldots$

✎ **Given the first term and the common ratio of a geometric sequence find the first five terms and the explicit formula.**

5) $a_1 = 0.4, r = -3$

6) $a_1 = 0.2, r = 4$

✎ **Given the recursive formula for a geometric sequence find the common ratio, the first five terms, and the explicit formula.**

7) $a_n = a_{n-1} \times 4, a_1 = 2$

8) $a_n = a_{n-1} \cdot (-2), a_1 = -4$

9) $a_n = a_{n-1} \cdot 5, a_1 = 0.2$

10) $a_n = a_{n-1} \cdot 3, a_1 = -3$

✎ **Given two terms in a geometric sequence find the 6th term and the recursive formula.**

11) $a_3 = 576$ and $a_5 = 36$

12) $a_2 = -0.4$ and $a_4 = -1.6$

WWW.MathNotion.Com

Algebra 2

Comparing Arithmetic and Geometric Sequences

✎ For each sequence, state if it is arithmetic, geometric, or neither.

1) 6, 11, 16, 21, …

2) 2, 5, 8, 11, …

3) 3, 10, 20, 27, …

4) 1, 11, 22, 33, 44, …

5) 4, 8, 10, 24, 96, …

6) 2, 10, 20, 50, 200, …

7) 0.2, 1, 5, 25, 125, …

8) 4, 12, 36, 108, …

9) −27, −34, −41, −48, −55, …

10) −3, 15, −75, 375, −1875, …

11) 10, 25, 50, 65, 80, …

12) 5, 15, 150, 250, 350 …

13) −35, −20, −5, 10, 25, …

14) $a_n = 4 \cdot 8^{n-1}$

15) $a_n = 3 \cdot 6^{n-1}$

16) $a_n = 8 - 4n$

17) $a_n = -210 + 310n$

18) $a_n = 53 + 53n$

19) $a_n = -10 \cdot (-5)^{n-1}$

20) $a_n = 49 + 63n$

21) $a_n = (3n)^4$

22) $a_n = 40 + 8n$

23) $a_n = -(13)^{n-1}$

24) $a_n = -10 \cdot (0.2)^{n-1}$

25) $a_n = \frac{3n+2}{4^n}$

26) $a_n = \frac{47+13n}{7n}$

27) $a_n = \frac{12-12n}{12n}$

28) $a_n = \frac{32 - a_{n-1}}{2n}$

29) $a_n = \frac{4}{15} - \frac{2}{7}n$

WWW.MathNotion.Com

Algebra 2

Finite Geometric Series

✎ **Evaluate the related series of each sequence.**

1) $-2, 4, -8, 16$

2) $-1, 6, -36, 216, -1,296$

3) $-2, 8, -32, 128, -512$

4) $4, 8, 16, 32, 64$

5) $-4, -12, -36, -108$

6) $5, -15, 45, -135, 405$

✎ **Evaluate each geometric series described.**

7) $1 + 5 + 25 + 125 \ldots, n = 5$ _____

8) $1 - 6 + 36 - 216 \ldots, n = 6$ _____

9) $-2 - 6 - 18 - 54 \ldots, n = 8$ _____

10) $0.2 - 1 + 5 - 25 \ldots, n = 6$ _____

11) $0.6 - 3.6 + 21.6 - 129.6 \ldots, n = 5$ _____

12) $-1 - 4 - 16 - 64 \ldots, n = 6$ _____

13) $a_1 = -2, r = 6, n = 5$ _____

14) $a_1 = 1, r = 9, n = 6$ _____

15) $\sum_{n=1}^{6} 4 \cdot (-3)^{n-1}$ _____

16) $\sum_{n=1}^{7} 2 \cdot (-5)^{n-1}$ _____

17) $\sum_{n=1}^{10} 0.1 \cdot (2)^{n-1}$ _____

18) $\sum_{m=1}^{6} (-4)^{m-1}$ _____

19) $\sum_{m=1}^{6} 5 \times (3)^{m-1}$ _____

20) $\sum_{k=1}^{5} 7 \times (6)^{k-1}$ _____

Algebra 2

Infinite Geometric Series

✎ **Determine if each geometric series converges or diverges.**

1) $a_1 = -1.8, r = 6$

2) $a_1 = 10.8, r = 0.3$

3) $a_1 = -2, r = 6.1$

4) $a_1 = 5, r = 0.24$

5) $a_1 = 1.2, r = 8$

6) $-1, 6, -36, 216, \ldots$

7) $6, -1, \frac{1}{6}, -\frac{1}{36}, \frac{1}{216}, \ldots$

8) $512 + 64 + 8 + 1 \ldots$

9) $-5 + \frac{15}{7} - \frac{45}{49} + \frac{135}{343} \ldots$

10) $\frac{400}{459} - \frac{200}{153} + \frac{100}{51} - \frac{50}{17} \ldots$

✎ **Evaluate each infinite geometric series described.**

11) $a_1 = 2, r = -\frac{1}{4}$

12) $a_1 = 36, r = -\frac{1}{6}$

13) $a_1 = 9, r = \frac{1}{3}$

14) $a_1 = 12, r = \frac{1}{7}$

15) $1 + 0.2 + 0.04 + 0.008 + \cdots$

16) $64 - 16 + 4 - 1 \ldots$,

17) $1 - 0.3 + 0.09 - 0.027 \ldots$,

18) $-5 + \frac{15}{7} - \frac{45}{49} + \frac{135}{343} \ldots$,

19) $\sum_{k=1}^{\infty} 7^{k-1}$

20) $\sum_{i=1}^{\infty} \left(\frac{2}{5}\right)^{i-1}$

21) $\sum_{k=1}^{\infty} \left(-\frac{2}{9}\right)^{k-1}$

22) $\sum_{n=1}^{\infty} 6\left(\frac{1}{3}\right)^{n-1}$

Algebra 2

Answers of Worksheets

Arithmetic Sequences

1) $2, -4, -10$
2) $-8, 4, 16$
3) $62, 71, 80$
4) $35, 41, 47$
5) First Five Terms: $20, 23, 26, 29, 32$, Explicit: $a_n = 20 + 3(n-1)$
6) First Five Terms: $-11, -16, -21, -26, -31$, Explicit: $a_n = -11 - 5(n-1)$
7) First Five Terms: $32, 38, 44, 50, 56$, Explicit: $a_n = 32 + 6(n-1)$
8) First Five Terms: $240, 160, 80, 0, -80$, Explicit: $a_n = 240 - 80(n-1)$
9) First Five Terms: $450, 400, 350, 300, 250$, Explicit: $a_n = 450 - 50(n-1)$
10) First Five Terms: $-63, -56, -49, -42, -35$, Explicit: $a_n = -63 + 7(n-1)$
11) First Five Terms: $171.8, 166.6, 161.4, 156.2, 151$, Explicit: $a_n = 171.8 - 5.2(n-1)$
12) First Five Terms: $829, 802, 775, 748, 721$, Explicit: $a_n = 829 - 27(n-1)$
13) Next 3 terms: $-196, -205, -214$, Recursive: $a_n = a_{n-1} - 9, a_1 = -7$
14) Next 3 terms: $68.7, 73.9, 79.1, 84.3$ Recursive: $a_n = a_{n-1} + 5.2, a_1 = 6.3$
15) Next 3 terms: $60, 61.8, 63.6$, Recursive: $a_n = a_{n-1} + 1.8, a_1 = 4.2$
16) Next 3 terms: $7.2, 7.6, 8$, Recursive: $a_n = a_{n-1} + 0.4, a_1 = -9.6$

Geometric Sequences

1) $r = -7$
2) $r = 4$
3) not geometric
4) $r = 2$
5) First Five Terms: $0.4, -1.2, 3.6, -10.8, 32.4$
   Explicit: $a_n = 0.4 \times (-3)^{n-1}$
6) First Five Terms: $0.2, 0.8, 3.2, 12.8, 51.2$
   Explicit: $a_n = 0.2 \times (4)^{n-1}$
7) Common Ratio: $r = 4$
   First Five Terms: $2, 8, 32, 128, 512$
   Explicit: $a_n = 2 \cdot (4)^{n-1}$

WWW.MathNotion.Com

Algebra 2

8) Common Ratio: $r = -2$

   First Five Terms: $-4, 8, -16, 32, -64$

   Explicit: $a_n = -4 \cdot (-2)^{n-1}$

9) Common Ratio: $r = 5$

   First Five Terms: $0.2, 1, 5, 25, 125, 625$

   Explicit: $a_n = 0.2 \cdot (5)^{n-1}$

10) Common Ratio: $r = 3$

    First Five Terms: $-3, -9, -27, -81, -243$

    Explicit: $a_n = -3 \cdot (3)^{n-1}$

11) $a_6 = -9$, Recursive: $a_n = a_{n-1} \cdot (\frac{-1}{4})$, $a_1 = 9,216$

12) $a_6 = -6.4$, Recursive: $a_n = a_{n-1} \cdot (-2)$, $a_1 = 0.2$

Comparing Arithmetic and Geometric Sequences

1) Arithmetic	11) Neither	21) Neither
2) Arithmetic	12) Neither	22) Arithmetic
3) Neither	13) Arithmetic	23) Geometric
4) Neither	14) Geometric	24) Geometric
5) Neither	15) Geometric	25) Neither
6) Neither	16) Arithmetic	26) Neither
7) Geometric	17) Arithmetic	27) Neither
8) Geometric	18) Arithmetic	28) Neither
9) Arithmetic	19) Geometric	29) Arithmetic
10) Geometric	20) Arithmetic	

Finite Geometric

1) 10	8) $-6,665$	15) -728
2) $-1,111$	9) $-6,560$	16) $26,042$
3) -410	10) -520.8	17) 102.3
4) 124	11) 666.6	18) -819
5) -160	12) $-1,365$	19) $1,820$
6) 305	13) $-3,110$	20) $10,885$
7) 781	14) $66,430$	

Algebra 2

Infinite Geometric

1) Diverges
2) Converges
3) Diverges
4) Converges
5) Diverges
6) Diverges
7) Converges
8) Converges
9) Converges
10) Converges
11) $\frac{8}{5}$
12) $\frac{216}{7}$
13) $\frac{27}{2}$
14) 14
15) $\frac{5}{4}$
16) $\frac{256}{5}$
17) $\frac{3}{4}$
18) $-\frac{7}{2}$
19) Infinite
20) $\frac{5}{3}$
21) $\frac{9}{11}$
22) 9

Algebra 2

Chapter 8 :
Rational Expressions

Topics that you will learn in this chapter:

- ✓ Simplifying and Graphing Rational Expressions
- ✓ Adding and Subtracting Rational Expressions
- ✓ Multiplying and Dividing Rational Expressions
- ✓ Solving Rational Equations and Complex Fractions

"What music is to the heart; mathematics is to the mind."
— Amit Kalantri

Algebra 2

Simplifying and Graphing Rational Expressions

✏️ **Simplify.**

1) $\dfrac{x+3}{3x+9} =$

2) $\dfrac{3x^2+12x+12}{x+2} =$

3) $\dfrac{8}{4x-4} =$

4) $\dfrac{x^2+6x+5}{x^2+9x+20} =$

5) $\dfrac{16x^4}{24x} =$

6) $\dfrac{x-1}{x^2+4x-5} =$

7) $\dfrac{x^2-5x-14}{x-7} =$

8) $\dfrac{36}{6x-6} =$

✏️ **Identify the points of discontinuity, holes, vertical asymptotes, x-intercepts, and horizontal asymptote of each.**

9) $f(x) = \dfrac{x^2-x+2}{-4x^2-4x+8} =$

10) $f(x) = \dfrac{-x-2}{-3x^2-15x-18} =$

11) $f(x) = \dfrac{x-2}{x-7} =$

12) $f(x) = \dfrac{3x^2}{3x^2-3x-6} =$

✏️ **Graph rational expressions.**

13) $f(x) = \dfrac{-x^2+3x-4}{x-3}$

14) $f(x) = \dfrac{-x^3-10x+32}{x^2-x-3}$

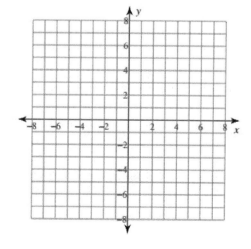
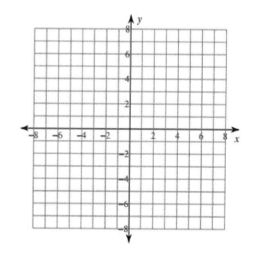

Algebra 2

Adding and Subtracting Rational Expressions

✎ **Simplify each expression.**

1) $\dfrac{3}{3x+7} + \dfrac{x-5}{3x+7} =$

2) $\dfrac{x+2}{x-2} + \dfrac{x-2}{x+5} =$

3) $\dfrac{2}{x+3} - \dfrac{5}{x-8} =$

4) $\dfrac{x-3}{x^2-11} - \dfrac{x-4}{11-x^2} =$

5) $\dfrac{2}{x+4} + \dfrac{6x}{3x+12} =$

6) $\dfrac{7+x}{2x} + \dfrac{x-3}{2x} =$

7) $3 + \dfrac{x-4}{x+3} =$

8) $\dfrac{3x}{3x+5} + \dfrac{5x}{4x+1} =$

9) $\dfrac{x+y}{y-x} - \dfrac{2xy}{y^2-x^2} =$

10) $\dfrac{3}{x^2-2x-8} + \dfrac{-3}{x^2-4} =$

11) $\dfrac{3}{x+4} - \dfrac{1}{x+2} =$

12) $\dfrac{4x+4}{4x^2+12x-16} + \dfrac{5x}{3x} =$

13) $2 + \dfrac{x}{x+2} - \dfrac{2}{x^2-4} =$

14) $\dfrac{3}{x+2} - \dfrac{3}{x+5} =$

15) $\dfrac{1}{5x^2+15x} + \dfrac{3}{2x} =$

16) $\dfrac{x^2+4x+4}{4x+8} + \dfrac{3x+3}{x+1} =$

17) $\dfrac{x}{3x+5} + \dfrac{3x}{3x+4} =$

18) $\dfrac{3}{12+4x} - \dfrac{3x-5}{4x^2+12x} =$

WWW.MathNotion.Com

Algebra 2

Multiplying and Dividing Rational Expressions

✎ Simplify each expression.

1) $\dfrac{10x}{15} \times \dfrac{15}{12x} =$

2) $\dfrac{63x}{12} \times \dfrac{60}{28x^2} =$

3) $\dfrac{75}{4} \times \dfrac{24x}{87} =$

4) $\dfrac{58}{27} \times \dfrac{27x^2}{43} =$

5) $\dfrac{90}{14x} \times \dfrac{32x}{45x} =$

6) $\dfrac{6x+30}{x+2} \times \dfrac{x+2}{6} =$

7) $\dfrac{x-9}{x+5} \times \dfrac{8x+40}{x-9} =$

8) $\dfrac{2}{x+11} \times \dfrac{5x+55}{5x+10} =$

9) $\dfrac{4(x+5)}{5x} \times \dfrac{9}{4(x+5)} =$

10) $\dfrac{7(x+3)}{x+3} \times \dfrac{7x}{7(x-5)} =$

11) $\dfrac{5x^2+10x}{x+6} \times \dfrac{1}{x+2} =$

12) $\dfrac{16x^2-16x}{14x^2-14x} \times \dfrac{6x}{6x^2} =$

13) $\dfrac{1}{x-7} \times \dfrac{x^2+4x-21}{x+7} =$

14) $\dfrac{x^2-12x+36}{12x-72} \times \dfrac{x-6}{36-6x} =$

✎ Divide.

15) $\dfrac{-1+2x-x^2}{x^2+4x-5} \div \dfrac{3x}{x+5} =$

16) $\dfrac{9a}{a+7} \div \dfrac{9a}{2a+14} =$

17) $\dfrac{13x}{x-9} \div \dfrac{13x}{8x-72} =$

18) $\dfrac{3x+12}{8x^2-80x} \div \dfrac{3}{8x} =$

19) $\dfrac{x-3}{x+3x-12} \div \dfrac{11x}{x+8} =$

20) $\dfrac{6x}{x-8} \div \dfrac{6x}{12x-96} =$

21) $\dfrac{x+6}{x^2+14x+48} \div \dfrac{5x}{x+8} =$

22) $\dfrac{x+2}{x^2+15x+54} \div \dfrac{5x}{x+9} =$

23) $\dfrac{16x+14}{4} \div \dfrac{64x+56}{4x} =$

24) $\dfrac{7x^3+49x^2}{x^2+16x+63} \div \dfrac{4(x+6)}{4x^3+24x^2} =$

25) $\dfrac{x^2+9x+14}{x^2+6x+8} \div \dfrac{1}{x+4} =$

26) $\dfrac{x^2+3x-10}{6x+30} \div \dfrac{3}{x+7} =$

27) $\dfrac{x+6}{x^2+10x+21} \div \dfrac{1}{x+7} =$

28) $\dfrac{1}{4x} \div \dfrac{8x}{2x^2+18x} =$

WWW.MathNotion.Com

Algebra 2

Solving Rational Equations and Complex Fractions

✏ **Solve each equation. Remember to check for extraneous solutions.**

1) $\dfrac{x-1}{x+3} = \dfrac{2x-2}{x-3}$

2) $\dfrac{1}{x} = \dfrac{5}{6x} + 2$

3) $\dfrac{3x-4}{6x+1} = \dfrac{x+4}{x-1}$

4) $\dfrac{1}{6b^2} + \dfrac{1}{6b} = \dfrac{1}{b^2}$

5) $\dfrac{2x-1}{5x+1} = \dfrac{3x-4}{x-7}$

6) $\dfrac{1}{3n^2} - \dfrac{1}{n} = \dfrac{1}{4n^2}$

7) $\dfrac{1}{8b^2} = \dfrac{1}{4b^2} - \dfrac{1}{2b}$

8) $\dfrac{1}{n-4} - 2 = \dfrac{3}{n-4}$

9) $\dfrac{4}{r-2} = -\dfrac{8}{r+2}$

10) $2 = \dfrac{2}{x^2+4x} + \dfrac{2x+2}{x}$

11) $\dfrac{3}{x} = 7 + \dfrac{2}{3x}$

12) $\dfrac{x+3}{x^2-x} - 2 = \dfrac{1}{x^2-x}$

13) $\dfrac{x-2}{x+5} - 1 = \dfrac{1}{x+2}$

14) $\dfrac{1}{12x^2} = \dfrac{1}{6x^2} - \dfrac{1}{2x}$

15) $\dfrac{x+3}{x^2+2x} = \dfrac{x}{x^2+2x} - \dfrac{6}{x+2}$

16) $1 = \dfrac{5}{2x^2+4x} + \dfrac{x+2}{2x}$

✏ **Simplify each expression.**

17) $\dfrac{\frac{3}{5}}{\frac{4}{45} - \frac{5}{18}} =$

18) $\dfrac{\frac{17}{2}}{-7\frac{4}{15}} =$

19) $\dfrac{7}{\frac{7}{x} + \frac{3}{4x}} =$

20) $\dfrac{2x^2}{\frac{3}{8} - \frac{3}{x}} =$

21) $\dfrac{\frac{2}{x-1} - \frac{1}{x+4}}{\frac{3}{x^2+9x+20}} =$

22) $\dfrac{\frac{14}{x-1}}{\frac{14}{7} - \frac{14}{42}} =$

23) $\dfrac{1 + \frac{8}{x-4}}{1 - \frac{4}{x-4}} =$

24) $\dfrac{\frac{1}{3} - \frac{x+2}{6}}{\frac{x^2}{4} - \frac{2}{3}} =$

WWW.MathNotion.Com

Algebra 2

Answers of Worksheets

Simplifying and Graphing rational expressions

1) $\frac{1}{3}$

2) $3(x+2)$

3) $\frac{2}{x-1}$

4) $\frac{x+1}{x+4}$

5) $\frac{2x^3}{3}$

6) $\frac{1}{x+5}$

7) $x+2$

8) $\frac{6}{x-1}$

9) Discontinuities: –2, 1;   Vertical Asymptote: $x=-2, x=1$;   Holes: None
   Horizontal. Asymptote: $y=-\frac{1}{4}$;   x–intercepts: None

10) Discontinuities –2, –3;   Vertical Asymptote $x=-3$;   Holes $x=-2$
    Horizontal Asymptote $y=0$;   x–intercepts. None

11) Discontinuities: 7;   Vertical Asymptote: $x=7$;   Holes: None
    Horizontal Asymptote: $y=1$;   x–intercepts: 2

12) Discontinuities: –1, 2;   Vertical Asymptote: $x=-1, x=2$;   Holes: None
    Horizontal Asymptote: $y=1$;   x–intercepts: 0

13)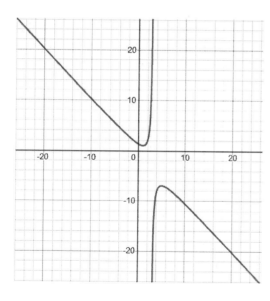

14)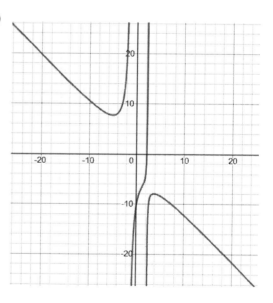

Adding and subtracting rational expressions

1) $\frac{x-2}{3x+7}$

2) $\frac{2x^2+3x+14}{(x-2)(x+5)}$

3) $\frac{-3x-31}{(x+3)(x-8)}$

4) $\frac{2x-7}{x^2-11}$

5) $\frac{2+2x}{x+4}$

6) $\frac{x+2}{x}$

7) $\frac{x-1}{x+3}$

8) $\frac{27x^2+28x}{(3x+5)(4x+1)}$

9) $\frac{x^2+y^2}{(x-y)(x+y)}$

Algebra 2

10) $\dfrac{6}{(x+2)(x-4)(x-2)}$

11) $\dfrac{2x+2}{(x+4)(x+2)}$

12) $\dfrac{5x^2+18x-17}{3(x-1)(x+4)}$

13) $\dfrac{3x^2-2x-10}{(x+2)(x-2)}$

14) $\dfrac{9}{(x+2)(x+5)}$

15) $\dfrac{15x+47}{10x(x+3)}$

16) $\dfrac{x+2}{4}+3$

17) $\dfrac{12x^2+19x}{(3x+5)(3x+4)}$

18) $\dfrac{5}{4x(x+3)}$

Multiplying and Dividing rational expressions

1) $\dfrac{5}{6}$

2) $\dfrac{45}{4x}$

3) $\dfrac{150x}{29}$

4) $\dfrac{58x^2}{43}$

5) $\dfrac{32}{7x}$

6) $x+5$

7) 8

8) $\dfrac{2}{x+2}$

9) $\dfrac{9}{5x}$

10) $\dfrac{7x}{x-5}$

11) $\dfrac{5x}{x+6}$

12) $\dfrac{8}{7x}$

13) $\dfrac{x-3}{x-7}$

14) $-\dfrac{(x-6)}{72}$

15) $-\dfrac{x-1}{3x}$

16) 2

17) 8

18) $\dfrac{x+4}{x-10}$

19) $\dfrac{x+8}{44x}$

20) 12

21) $\dfrac{1}{5x}$

22) $\dfrac{x+2}{5x(x+6)}$

23) $\dfrac{x}{4}$

24) $\dfrac{7x^4}{x+9}$

25) $x+7$

26) $\dfrac{(x-2)(x+7)}{18}$

27) $\dfrac{x+6}{x+3}$

28) $\dfrac{x+9}{16x}$

Solving rational equations and complex fractions

1) $\{1,-9\}$

2) $\{\dfrac{1}{12}\}$

3) $\{\dfrac{-32}{3}, 0\}$

4) $\{5\}$

5) $\{-\dfrac{11}{13}, 1\}$

6) $\{\dfrac{1}{12}\}$

7) $\{\dfrac{1}{4}\}$

8) $\{3\}$

9) $\{\dfrac{2}{3}\}$

10) $\{-5\}$

11) $\{\dfrac{1}{3}\}$

12) $\{2, -\dfrac{1}{2}\}$

13) $\{-\dfrac{19}{8}\}$

14) $\{\dfrac{1}{6}\}$

15) $\{-\dfrac{1}{2}\}$

16) $\{3, -3\}$

17) $-\dfrac{54}{17}$

18) $-1\dfrac{37}{218}$

19) $\dfrac{28x}{31}$

20) $\dfrac{16x^3}{3x-24}$

21) $\dfrac{(x+9)(x+5)}{3(x-1)}$

22) $\dfrac{42}{5(x-1)}$

23) $\dfrac{x+4}{x-8}$

24) $-\dfrac{2x}{3x^2-8}$

Algebra 2

Chapter 9 :
Matrices

Topics that you will practice in this chapter:

✓ Adding and Subtracting Matrices
✓ Matrix Multiplications
✓ Finding Determinants of a Matrix
✓ Finding Inverse of a Matrix
✓ Matrix Equations

Mathematics is an independent world created out of pure intelligence.
− *William Woods Worth*

Algebra 2

Adding and Subtracting Matrices

✎ **Simplify.**

1) $\begin{vmatrix} -4 & 3 & -4 \end{vmatrix} + \begin{vmatrix} 0 & -3 & -3 \end{vmatrix}$

2) $\begin{vmatrix} 4 & 3 \\ -1 & -5 \\ -6 & 1 \end{vmatrix} + \begin{vmatrix} 1 & -4 \\ 1 & 5 \\ 6 & 2 \end{vmatrix}$

3) $\begin{vmatrix} -2 & 2 & -4 \\ 4 & -2 & -1 \end{vmatrix} - \begin{vmatrix} 6 & 0 & -4 \\ 1 & 4 & -4 \end{vmatrix}$

4) $\begin{vmatrix} 6 & 2 \end{vmatrix} + \begin{vmatrix} -3 & -7 \end{vmatrix}$

5) $\begin{vmatrix} 3 \\ 2 \end{vmatrix} + \begin{vmatrix} 5 \\ 8 \end{vmatrix}$

6) $\begin{vmatrix} -4r + 5t \\ -2r \\ 3s \end{vmatrix} + \begin{vmatrix} 4r \\ -3t \\ -7r + 1 \end{vmatrix}$

7) $\begin{vmatrix} 3z - 4 \\ -8 \\ -2 - 5z \\ 3y \end{vmatrix} + \begin{vmatrix} -y \\ 3z \\ 6 + z \\ 7z \end{vmatrix}$

8) $\begin{vmatrix} -2n & 3n + m \\ -4n & -7m \end{vmatrix} + \begin{vmatrix} 5 & -4 \\ 2m & m \end{vmatrix}$

9) $\begin{vmatrix} 3 & 8 \\ -6 & 4 \end{vmatrix} - \begin{vmatrix} 2 & -3 \\ 4 & 11 \end{vmatrix}$

10) $\begin{vmatrix} 0 & -2 & 3 \\ 2 & -3 & 4 \\ -7 & 3 & -8 \end{vmatrix} + \begin{vmatrix} -5 & 8 & -9 \\ 7 & 2 & 7 \\ 5 & -5 & -6 \end{vmatrix}$

WWW.MathNotion.Com

Algebra 2

Matrix Multiplication

✎ **Simplify.**

1) $\begin{vmatrix} -3 & -3 \\ -2 & 2 \end{vmatrix} \times \begin{vmatrix} -2 & -4 \\ 4 & 1 \end{vmatrix}$

2) $\begin{vmatrix} 2 & 0 \\ -2 & 1 \\ -1 & 2 \end{vmatrix} \times \begin{vmatrix} -2 & 5 \\ 1 & -2 \end{vmatrix}$

3) $\begin{vmatrix} 4 & 2 & 1 \\ 1 & 5 & 0 \end{vmatrix} \times \begin{vmatrix} 1 & 4 & 2 \\ 3 & -1 & 3 \end{vmatrix}$

4) $\begin{vmatrix} -7 \\ 2 \\ 4 \end{vmatrix} \times \begin{vmatrix} 1 & -5 \end{vmatrix}$

5) $\begin{vmatrix} 4 & -3 \\ 2 & 0 \\ 1 & -2 \end{vmatrix} \times \begin{vmatrix} -1 & 1 \\ 5 & 3 \end{vmatrix}$

6) $\begin{vmatrix} 2 & 2 \\ -2 & 1 \end{vmatrix} \cdot \begin{vmatrix} 6 & -2 \\ 0 & 3 \end{vmatrix}$

7) $\begin{vmatrix} -2 & -y \\ 2x & -3 \end{vmatrix} \cdot \begin{vmatrix} -x & 3 \\ -2y & -2 \end{vmatrix}$

8) $\begin{vmatrix} 3 & -2v \end{vmatrix} \cdot \begin{vmatrix} -2u & -v \\ 0 & 1 \end{vmatrix}$

9) $\begin{vmatrix} -3 & 1 & 1 \\ 1 & 0 & -2 \\ 2 & -1 & 2 \\ -4 & 1 & 0 \end{vmatrix} \cdot \begin{vmatrix} 3 & 1 \\ 1 & -1 \\ 4 & 3 \end{vmatrix}$

10) $\begin{vmatrix} 1 & 0 & 3 \\ 2 & 1 & 0 \end{vmatrix} \cdot \begin{vmatrix} -2 & 1 \\ -2 & 2 \\ 4 & -3 \end{vmatrix}$

11) $\begin{vmatrix} -1 & 0 \\ -4 & 5 \end{vmatrix} \cdot \begin{vmatrix} 1 & -1 \\ 2 & 5 \end{vmatrix}$

12) $\begin{vmatrix} 3 & 1 \\ -2 & -1 \end{vmatrix} \cdot \begin{vmatrix} 0 & -3 \\ 5 & 5 \end{vmatrix}$

13) $\begin{vmatrix} 2 & 1 \\ -2 & -4 \end{vmatrix} \cdot \begin{vmatrix} 0 & -2 \\ 1 & 2 \end{vmatrix}$

14) $\begin{vmatrix} -3 & -3 \\ 2 & 1 \\ 0 & 1 \\ 0 & -2 \end{vmatrix} \times \begin{vmatrix} 3 & -2 & 3 \\ -2 & 1 & -2 \end{vmatrix}$

WWW.MathNotion.Com

Algebra 2

Finding Determinants of a Matrix

✎ **Evaluate the determinant of each matrix.**

1) $\begin{vmatrix} 3 & 9 \\ 0 & -8 \end{vmatrix}$

2) $\begin{vmatrix} 8 & 4 \\ 3 & 2 \end{vmatrix}$

3) $\begin{vmatrix} -3 & 4 \\ 5 & 5 \end{vmatrix}$

4) $\begin{vmatrix} -2 & 1 \\ -3 & 6 \end{vmatrix}$

5) $\begin{vmatrix} -4 & 3 \\ 3 & 2 \end{vmatrix}$

6) $\begin{vmatrix} 8 & -2 \\ 1 & 5 \end{vmatrix}$

7) $\begin{vmatrix} 2 & -8 \\ 0 & -9 \end{vmatrix}$

8) $\begin{vmatrix} 8 & 7 \\ 5 & 6 \end{vmatrix}$

9) $\begin{vmatrix} 3 & 6 \\ -7 & 2 \end{vmatrix}$

10) $\begin{vmatrix} 4 & 0 \\ 5 & 8 \end{vmatrix}$

11) $\begin{vmatrix} 3 & -2 & 0 \\ 1 & 2 & -1 \\ 3 & 2 & 2 \end{vmatrix}$

12) $\begin{vmatrix} -3 & 0 & -3 \\ -3 & 1 & 2 \\ 2 & 2 & 1 \end{vmatrix}$

13) $\begin{vmatrix} 2 & 1 & 4 \\ 5 & -5 & 1 \\ 1 & 0 & 2 \end{vmatrix}$

14) $\begin{vmatrix} 1 & -2 & 4 \\ 2 & 3 & -1 \\ 3 & 2 & 0 \end{vmatrix}$

15) $\begin{vmatrix} 2 & 0 & 1 \\ 1 & -1 & -1 \\ 2 & 3 & 0 \end{vmatrix}$

Algebra 2

Finding Inverse of a Matrix

✍ **Find the inverse of each matrix.**

1) $\begin{vmatrix} 2 & 7 \\ 2 & 9 \end{vmatrix}$

2) $\begin{vmatrix} 6 & 17 \\ 1 & 3 \end{vmatrix}$

3) $\begin{vmatrix} 3 & 3 \\ 3 & 4 \end{vmatrix}$

4) $\begin{vmatrix} 7 & 1 \\ 3 & 2 \end{vmatrix}$

5) $\begin{vmatrix} -2 & 5 \\ 4 & 1 \end{vmatrix}$

6) $\begin{vmatrix} 6 & 3 \\ 5 & 5 \end{vmatrix}$

7) $\begin{vmatrix} 2 & 8 \\ 0 & 3 \end{vmatrix}$

8) $\begin{vmatrix} -5 & -3 \\ 2 & 3 \end{vmatrix}$

9) $\begin{vmatrix} -3 & 6 \\ -4 & 8 \end{vmatrix}$

10) $\begin{vmatrix} -2 & 3 \\ 3 & 5 \end{vmatrix}$

11) $\begin{vmatrix} 7 & 5 \\ 9 & 8 \end{vmatrix}$

12) $\begin{vmatrix} 0 & 7 \\ 5 & 4 \end{vmatrix}$

13) $\begin{vmatrix} 0 & 0 \\ 7 & 8 \end{vmatrix}$

14) $\begin{vmatrix} 12 & 8 \\ 6 & 4 \end{vmatrix}$

Algebra 2

Matrix Equations

✎ **Solve each equation.**

1) $\begin{vmatrix} -1 & 3 \\ 2 & 0 \end{vmatrix} z = \begin{vmatrix} 10 \\ 4 \end{vmatrix}$

2) $4x = \begin{vmatrix} 16 & -4 \\ 8 & -20 \end{vmatrix}$

3) $\begin{vmatrix} -3 & 7 \\ -8 & 6 \end{vmatrix} = \begin{vmatrix} 2 & 8 \\ 1 & 3 \end{vmatrix} - x$

4) $Y - \begin{vmatrix} -2 \\ -6 \\ 10 \\ 7 \end{vmatrix} = \begin{vmatrix} -2 \\ 14 \\ -12 \\ -4 \end{vmatrix}$

5) $\begin{vmatrix} -3 & -4 \\ 2 & -5 \end{vmatrix} C = \begin{vmatrix} -10 \\ -24 \end{vmatrix}$

6) $\begin{vmatrix} -2 & -3 \\ 5 & 4 \end{vmatrix} B = \begin{vmatrix} -4 & 1 & -2 \\ 3 & 8 & -2 \end{vmatrix}$

7) $\begin{vmatrix} -4 & 6 \\ 2 & -3 \end{vmatrix} C = \begin{vmatrix} 28 \\ -14 \end{vmatrix}$

8) $\begin{vmatrix} 3 & 4 \\ 5 & 2 \end{vmatrix} C = \begin{vmatrix} 6 \\ -4 \end{vmatrix}$

9) $\begin{vmatrix} 4 & -3 \\ 0 & 5 \end{vmatrix} Z = \begin{vmatrix} 32 \\ -20 \end{vmatrix}$

10) $\begin{vmatrix} -10 \\ 5 \\ -25 \end{vmatrix} = 5B$

11) $\begin{vmatrix} -9 \\ 6 \\ 8 \end{vmatrix} = y - \begin{vmatrix} 11 \\ -3 \\ -7 \end{vmatrix}$

12) $-6b - \begin{vmatrix} 12 \\ 6 \\ -12 \end{vmatrix} = \begin{vmatrix} -18 \\ -24 \\ -36 \end{vmatrix}$

Algebra 2

Answers of Worksheets

Adding and Subtracting Matrices

1) $\begin{vmatrix} -4 & 0 & -7 \end{vmatrix}$

2) $\begin{vmatrix} 5 & -1 \\ 0 & 0 \\ 0 & 3 \end{vmatrix}$

3) $\begin{vmatrix} -8 & 2 & 0 \\ 3 & -6 & 3 \end{vmatrix}$

4) $\begin{vmatrix} 3 & -5 \end{vmatrix}$

5) $\begin{vmatrix} 8 \\ 10 \end{vmatrix}$

6) $\begin{vmatrix} 5t \\ -2r - 3t \\ 3s - 7r + 1 \end{vmatrix}$

7) $\begin{vmatrix} 3z - 4 - y \\ -8 + 3z \\ 4 - 4z \\ 3y + 7z \end{vmatrix}$

8) $\begin{vmatrix} -2n + 5 & 2n + m - 4 \\ -4n + 2m & -6m \end{vmatrix}$

9) $\begin{vmatrix} 1 & 11 \\ -10 & -7 \end{vmatrix}$

10) $\begin{vmatrix} -5 & 6 & -6 \\ 9 & -1 & 11 \\ -2 & -2 & -14 \end{vmatrix}$

Matrix Multiplication

1) $\begin{vmatrix} -6 & 9 \\ 12 & 10 \end{vmatrix}$

2) $\begin{vmatrix} -4 & 10 \\ 5 & -12 \\ 4 & -9 \end{vmatrix}$

3) Undefined

4) $\begin{vmatrix} -7 & 35 \\ 2 & -10 \\ 4 & -20 \end{vmatrix}$

5) $\begin{vmatrix} -19 & -5 \\ -2 & 2 \\ -11 & -5 \end{vmatrix}$

6) $\begin{vmatrix} 12 & 2 \\ -12 & 7 \end{vmatrix}$

7) $\begin{vmatrix} 2x + 2y^2 & 2y - 6 \\ -2x^2 + 6y & 6x + 6 \end{vmatrix}$

8) $\begin{vmatrix} -6u & -5v \end{vmatrix}$

9) $\begin{vmatrix} -4 & -1 \\ -5 & -5 \\ 13 & 9 \\ -11 & -5 \end{vmatrix}$

10) $\begin{vmatrix} 10 & -8 \\ -6 & 4 \end{vmatrix}$

11) $\begin{vmatrix} -1 & 1 \\ 6 & 29 \end{vmatrix}$

12) $\begin{vmatrix} 5 & -4 \\ -5 & 1 \end{vmatrix}$

13) $\begin{vmatrix} 1 & -2 \\ -4 & -4 \end{vmatrix}$

14) $\begin{vmatrix} -3 & 3 & -3 \\ 4 & -3 & 4 \\ -2 & 1 & -2 \\ 4 & -2 & 4 \end{vmatrix}$

Finding Determinants of a Matrix

1) –24
2) 4
3) –35
4) –9
5) –17
6) 42
7) –18
8) 13
9) 48

WWW.MathNotion.Com

Algebra 2

10) 32
11) 28
12) 33
13) −9
14) −12
15) 11

Finding Inverse of a Matrix

1) $\begin{vmatrix} \frac{9}{4} & \frac{-7}{4} \\ \frac{-1}{2} & \frac{1}{2} \end{vmatrix}$

2) $\begin{vmatrix} 3 & -17 \\ -1 & 6 \end{vmatrix}$

3) $\begin{vmatrix} \frac{4}{3} & -1 \\ -1 & 1 \end{vmatrix}$

4) $\begin{vmatrix} \frac{2}{11} & \frac{-1}{11} \\ \frac{-3}{11} & \frac{7}{11} \end{vmatrix}$

5) $\begin{vmatrix} -\frac{1}{22} & \frac{5}{22} \\ \frac{2}{11} & \frac{1}{11} \end{vmatrix}$

6) $\begin{vmatrix} \frac{1}{3} & -\frac{1}{5} \\ -\frac{1}{3} & \frac{2}{5} \end{vmatrix}$

7) $\begin{vmatrix} \frac{1}{2} & -\frac{4}{3} \\ 0 & \frac{1}{3} \end{vmatrix}$

8) $\begin{vmatrix} -\frac{1}{3} & -\frac{1}{3} \\ \frac{2}{9} & \frac{5}{9} \end{vmatrix}$

9) No inverse exists

10) $\begin{vmatrix} -\frac{5}{19} & \frac{3}{19} \\ \frac{3}{19} & \frac{2}{19} \end{vmatrix}$

11) $\begin{vmatrix} \frac{8}{11} & -\frac{5}{11} \\ -\frac{9}{11} & \frac{7}{11} \end{vmatrix}$

12) $\begin{vmatrix} -\frac{4}{35} & \frac{1}{5} \\ \frac{1}{7} & 0 \end{vmatrix}$

13) No inverse exists.

14) No inverse exists.

Matrix Equations

1) $\begin{vmatrix} 2 \\ 4 \end{vmatrix}$

2) $\begin{vmatrix} 4 & -1 \\ 2 & -5 \end{vmatrix}$

3) $\begin{vmatrix} 5 & 1 \\ -7 & -3 \end{vmatrix}$

4) $\begin{vmatrix} -4 \\ 8 \\ -2 \\ 3 \end{vmatrix}$

5) $\begin{vmatrix} -2 \\ 4 \end{vmatrix}$

6) $\begin{vmatrix} -1 & 4 & -2 \\ 2 & -3 & 2 \end{vmatrix}$

7) $\begin{vmatrix} -1 \\ 4 \end{vmatrix}$

8) $\begin{vmatrix} -2 \\ 3 \end{vmatrix}$

9) $\begin{vmatrix} 5 \\ -4 \end{vmatrix}$

10) $\begin{vmatrix} -2 \\ 1 \\ -5 \end{vmatrix}$

11) $\begin{vmatrix} 2 \\ 3 \\ 1 \end{vmatrix}$

12) $\begin{vmatrix} 1 \\ 3 \\ 8 \end{vmatrix}$

Algebra 2

Chapter 10:
Logarithms

Topics that you'll practice in this chapter:

- ✓ Rewriting Logarithms
- ✓ Evaluating Logarithms
- ✓ Properties of Logarithms
- ✓ Natural Logarithms
- ✓ Exponential Equations Requiring Logarithms
- ✓ Solving Logarithmic Equations

Mathematics is an art of human understanding. — *William Thurston*

Algebra 2

Rewriting Logarithms

✎ **Rewrite each equation in exponential form.**

1) $\log_3 27 = 3$

2) $\log_2 128 = 7$

3) $\log_6 1,296 = 4$

4) $\log_5 625 = 4$

5) $\log_{11} 121 = 2$

6) $\log_{12} 1,728 = 3$

7) $\log_9 729 = 3$

8) $\log_3 729 = 6$

9) $\log_{10} 10,000 = 4$

10) $\log_7 343 = 3$

11) $\log_4 1,024 = 5$

12) $\log_{12} 144 = 2$

13) $\log_{13} 2,197 = 3$

14) $\log_{25} 5 = \frac{1}{2}$

15) $\log_{81} 3 = \frac{1}{4}$

16) $\log_{3,125} 5 = \frac{1}{5}$

17) $\log_{1,000} 10 = \frac{1}{3}$

18) $\log_5 \frac{1}{125} = -3$

19) $\log_4 \frac{1}{16} = -2$

20) $\log_a \frac{7}{4} = b$

✎ **Rewrite each exponential equation in logarithmic form.**

21) $2^5 = 32$

22) $4^3 = 64$

23) $5^4 = 625$

24) $11^3 = 1,331$

25) $3^5 = 243$

26) $6^4 = 1,296$

27) $7^4 = 2,401$

28) $9^3 = 729$

29) $4^{-5} = \frac{1}{1,024}$

30) $3^{-8} = \frac{1}{6,561}$

31) $11^{-2} = \frac{1}{121}$

32) $12^{-3} = \frac{1}{1,728}$

33) $4^{-5} = \frac{1}{1,024}$

34) $10^{-5} = \frac{1}{100,000}$

Algebra 2

Evaluating Logarithms

✎ **Evaluate each logarithm.**

1) $\log_3 729 =$

2) $\log_2 256 =$

3) $\log_3 243 =$

4) $\log_4 64 =$

5) $\log_8 64 =$

6) $\log_{11} 121 =$

7) $\log_{10} 10,000 =$

8) $\log_5 \frac{1}{25} =$

9) $\log_4 \frac{1}{256} =$

10) $\log_2 \frac{1}{32} =$

11) $\log_6 \frac{1}{36} =$

12) $\log_9 \frac{1}{81} =$

13) $\log_{12} \frac{1}{144} =$

14) $\log_{1,000} \frac{1}{10} =$

15) $\log_{243} 3 =$

16) $\log_4 \frac{1}{16} =$

17) $\log_8 \frac{1}{512} =$

18) $\log_3 \frac{1}{81} =$

✎ **Circle the points which are on the graph of the given logarithmic functions.**

19) $y = 4\log_4(3x - 2) + 1$ $(3, 4),$ $(2, 5),$ $(7, 4)$

20) $y = 5\log_6(12x) - 7$ $(2, -2),$ $(\frac{1}{3}, 12),$ $(\frac{1}{2}, -2)$

21) $y = -2\log_3 9(x - 5) + 5$ $(6, -3),$ $(8, -1),$ $(1, 6)$

22) $y = \frac{1}{4}\log_6(6x) + \frac{1}{2}$ $(6, 1),$ $(6, \frac{1}{4}),$ $(4, \frac{1}{4})$

23) $y = -2\log_8 8(x + 4) + 9$ $(-4, 0),$ $(0, 9),$ $(-2, 6\frac{1}{3})$

24) $y = -\log_5(x + 15) - 6$ $(10, -\frac{1}{5}),$ $(10, -8),$ $(11, -\frac{2}{5})$

25) $y = -3\log_2(2x + 6) + 7$ $(5, -5),$ $(-5, -5),$ $(-2, -2)$

Algebra 2

Properties of Logarithms

✎ **Expand each logarithm.**

1) $\log(11 \times 4) =$

2) $\log(13 \times 5) =$

3) $\log(4 \times 12) =$

4) $\log\left(\frac{2}{7}\right) =$

5) $\log\left(\frac{4}{9}\right) =$

6) $\log\left(\frac{5}{8}\right)^3 =$

7) $\log(6 \times 5^4) =$

8) $\log\left(\frac{14}{3}\right)^5 =$

9) $\log\left(\frac{3^4}{8}\right) =$

10) $\log(x \times y)^8 =$

11) $\log(x^6 \times y^{12} \times z^2) =$

12) $\log\left(\frac{u^8}{v^3}\right) =$

13) $\log\left(\frac{x}{y^7}\right) =$

✎ **Condense each expression to a single logarithm.**

14) $\log 8 - \log 13 =$

15) $\log 6 + \log 11 =$

16) $4\log 2 - 7\log 5 =$

17) $10\log 4 - 3\log 7 =$

18) $3\log 9 - \log 17 =$

19) $11\log 6 - 9\log 4 =$

20) $\log 15 - 6\log 7 =$

21) $6\log 8 + 4\log 10 =$

22) $12\log 5 + 14\log 9 =$

23) $17\log_8 a + 6\log_8 b =$

24) $2\log_9 x - 3\log_9 y =$

25) $\log_{11} u - 16\log_{11} v =$

26) $8\log_{15} u + 9\log_{15} v =$

27) $32\log_6 u - 25\log_6 v =$

WWW.MathNotion.Com

Algebra 2

Natural Logarithms

✍ **Solve each equation for** x.

1) $e^x = 9$

2) $e^x = 36$

3) $e^x = 49$

4) $\ln x = 3$

5) $\ln(\ln x) = 7$

6) $e^x = 4$

7) $\ln(5x + 2) = 1$

8) $\ln(7x + 4) = 3$

9) $\ln(9x + 5) = 4$

10) $\ln x = \frac{1}{9}$

11) $\ln 11x = e^5$

12) $\ln x = \ln 6 + \ln 7$

13) $\ln x = 4\ln 3 + \ln 2$

✍ **Evaluate without using a calculator.**

14) $11 \ln e =$

15) $\ln e^{10} =$

16) $4 \ln e =$

17) $\ln e^{21} =$

18) $32 \ln e =$

19) $4 \ln e^5 =$

20) $e^{\ln 22} =$

21) $e^{3\ln 3} =$

22) $e^{3\ln 5} =$

23) $\ln \sqrt[11]{e} =$

✍ **Reduce the following expressions to simplest form.**

24) $e^{-4\ln 9 + 4\ln 3} =$

25) $e^{-3\ln\left(\frac{5}{4e}\right)} =$

26) $2 \ln(e^4) =$

27) $\ln\left(\frac{1}{e}\right)^4 =$

28) $e^{\ln 9 + 3\ln 3} =$

29) $e^{\ln\left(\frac{13}{e}\right)} =$

30) $8 \ln(1^{-3e}) =$

31) $2 \ln\left(\frac{1}{e}\right)^{-3} =$

32) $6 \ln\left(\frac{\sqrt[3]{e}}{3e}\right) =$

33) $e^{-4\ln e + 2\ln 5} =$

34) $e^{\ln\frac{4}{e}} =$

35) $11 \ln(e^e) =$

Algebra 2

Exponential Equations and Logarithms

✎ **Solve each equation for the unknown variable.**

1) $3^{4n} = 243$

2) $5^{3r} = 625$

3) $6^{2n-1} = 216$

4) $16^{2r+3} = 4$

5) $169^{2x} = 13$

6) $7^{-3v-3} = 49$

7) $2^{4n} = 128$

8) $11^{n-1} = 1{,}331$

9) $\dfrac{9^{3a}}{3^{2a}} = 729$

10) $13^5 \times 13^{-4v} = 169$

11) $4^{3n} = \dfrac{1}{64}$

12) $\left(\dfrac{1}{11}\right)^{2n} = 121$

13) $2{,}187^{3x} = 3$

14) $13^{5-7x} = 13^{-2x}$

15) $11^{-3x} = 11^{2x-7}$

16) $3^{5n} = 243$

17) $17^{5x+3} = 17^{6x}$

18) $15^{3n} = 225$

19) $4^{-3k} = 512$

20) $8^{-4r} = 8^{-5r+2}$

21) $8^{2x+3} = 8^{5x}$

22) $10^{3x-2} = 100{,}000$

23) $16 \times 64^{-v} = 128$

24) $\dfrac{128}{2^{-3m}} = 2^{4m+5}$

25) $14^{-5n} \times 14^{2n+3} = 14^{-2n}$

26) $\left(\dfrac{1}{9}\right)^{4n+3} \times \left(\dfrac{1}{9}\right)^{-3n-8} = \left(\dfrac{1}{9}\right)^{-4n}$

✎ **Solve each problem. (Round to the nearest whole number)**

27) A substance decays 16% each day. After 8 days, there are 6 milligrams of the substance remaining. How many milligrams were there initially? _____

28) A culture of bacteria grows continuously. The culture doubles every 4 hours. If the initial number of bacteria is 20, how many bacteria will there be in 13 hours? _____

29) Bob plans to invest $11,200 at an annual rate of 3.5%. How much will Bob have in the account after three years if the balance is compounded quarterly? _____

30) Suppose you plan to invest $8,000 at an annual rate of 5%. How much will you have in the account after 6 years if the balance is compounded monthly? _____

Algebra 2

Solving Logarithmic Equations

✎ **Find the value of the variables in each equation.**

1) $2\log(x) + 5 = 9$

2) $\log_4 4x + 3 = 5$

3) $-\log_8(8x) + 2 = 3$

4) $\log 2x - \log 4 = 1$

5) $\log 5x + \log 25 = 1$

6) $\log 4 - \log x = 3$

7) $\log 4x + \log 2 = \log 16$

8) $-6\log_3(5x - 1) = -36$

9) $\log 4x = \log(8x - 1)$

10) $\log(4k - 6) = \log(k - 3)$

11) $\log(5p + 2) = \log(p + 4)$

12) $-30 + \log_4(3n + 2) = -30$

13) $\log_4(4x - 4) = \log_4(x^2)$

14) $\log_8(k^2 + 15) = \log_8(-6k - 3)$

15) $\log(16 + 6b) = \log(10b^2 + 12b)$

16) $\log_6(2x + 5) - \log_6 x = \log_6 9$

17) $\log_5 5 + \log_5(x^2 + 1) = \log_5 25$

18) $\log_6(x + 3) + \log_6(x + 1) = \log_6 8$

✎ **Find the value of x in each natural logarithm equation.**

19) $\ln 8 - \ln(4x + 8) = 4$

20) $\ln(x + 5) - \ln(x + 2) = \ln 10$

21) $\ln e^6 - \ln(x - 1) = 3$

22) $\ln(2x - 8) + \ln(x - 4) = \ln 8$

23) $\ln 5x - \ln(x + 4) = \ln 2$

24) $\ln(8x - 4) - \ln(x - 2) = \ln 25$

25) $\ln(3x + 2) - 4\ln 2 = 5$

26) $\ln(2x - 5) + \ln(x - 3) = \ln 6$

27) $\ln(x - 1) + \ln(4x - 7) = \ln(7)$

28) $2\ln 3x - \ln(x + 10) = \ln 2x$

29) $\ln x^4 + \ln x^8 = 4\ln(2x)$

30) $\ln x^{10} - \ln(x^2 + 10) = 10\ln 2x$

31) $8\ln(x - 2) = 4\ln(x^2 - 4x + 4)$

32) $\ln(x^4 + 10) = \ln(x^2 + 9)$

33) $2\ln x - 2\ln(x + 8) = \ln(x^2)$

34) $\ln(2x + 1) - \ln(4x + 1) = \ln 4$

35) $\ln 16 + 2\ln(x - 2) = \ln 4$

36) $\ln e^2 + \ln(5x - 6) = \ln(5) + 3$

WWW.MathNotion.Com

Algebra 2

Answers of Worksheets

Rewriting Logarithms

1) $3^3 = 27$
2) $2^7 = 128$
3) $6^4 = 1,296$
4) $5^4 = 625$
5) $11^2 = 121$
6) $12^3 = 1,728$
7) $9^3 = 729$
8) $3^6 = 729$
9) $10^4 = 10,000$
10) $7^3 = 343$
11) $4^5 = 1,024$
12) $12^2 = 144$
13) $13^3 = 2,197$

14) $25^{\frac{1}{2}} = 5$
15) $81^{\frac{1}{4}} = 3$
16) $3,125^{\frac{1}{5}} = 5$
17) $1,000^{\frac{1}{3}} = 10$
18) $5^{-3} = \frac{1}{125}$
19) $4^{-2} = \frac{1}{16}$
20) $a^b = \frac{7}{4}$
21) $\log_2 32 = 5$
22) $\log_4 64 = 3$
23) $\log_5 625 = 4$
24) $\log_{11} 1,331 = 3$

25) $\log_3 243 = 5$
26) $\log_6 1,296 = 4$
27) $\log_7 2,401 = 4$
28) $\log_9 729 = 3$
29) $\log_4 \frac{1}{1,024} = -5$
30) $\log_3 \frac{1}{6,561} = -8$
31) $\log_{11} \frac{1}{121} = -2$
32) $\log_{12} \frac{1}{1,728} = -3$
33) $\log_4 \frac{1}{1,024} = -5$
34) $\log_{10} \frac{1}{100,000} = -5$

Evaluating Logarithms

1) 6
2) 8
3) 5
4) 3
5) 2
6) 2
7) 4
8) -2
9) -4

10) -5
11) -2
12) -2
13) -2
14) $-\frac{1}{3}$
15) $\frac{1}{5}$
16) -2
17) -3

18) -4
19) $(2, 5)$
20) $(\frac{1}{2}, -2)$
21) $(8, -1)$
22) $(6, 1)$
23) $(-2, 6\frac{1}{3})$
24) $(10, -8)$
25) $(5, -5)$

Properties of Logarithms

1) $\log 11 + \log 4$
2) $\log 13 + \log 5$
3) $\log 4 + \log 12$
4) $\log 2 - \log 7$
5) $\log 4 - \log 9$
6) $3 \log 5 - 3 \log 8$
7) $\log 6 + 4 \log 5$
8) $5 \log 14 - 5 \log 3$

Algebra 2

9) $4\log 3 - \log 8$

10) $8\log x + 8\log y$

11) $6\log x + 12\log y + 2\log z$

12) $8\log u - 3\log v$

13) $\log x - 7\log y$

14) $\log \frac{8}{13}$

15) $\log(6 \times 11)$

16) $\log \frac{2^4}{5^7}$

17) $\log \frac{4^{10}}{7^3}$

18) $\log \frac{9^3}{17}$

19) $\log \frac{6^{11}}{4^9}$

20) $\log \frac{15}{7^6}$

21) $\log (8^6 \times 10^4)$

22) $\log (5^{12} \times 9^{14})$

23) $\log_8 (a^{17}b^6)$

24) $\log_9 \frac{x^2}{y^3}$

25) $\log_{11} \frac{u}{v^{16}}$

26) $\log_{15}(u^8 \times v^9)$

27) $\log_6 \frac{u^{32}}{v^{25}}$

Natural Logarithms

1) $x = \ln 9$

2) $x = \ln 36, x = 2\ln (6)$

3) $x = \ln 49, x = 2\ln (7)$

4) $x = e^3$

5) $x = e^{e^7}$

6) $x = \ln 4$

7) $x = \frac{e-2}{5}$

8) $x = \frac{e^3-4}{7}$

9) $x = \frac{e^4-5}{9}$

10) $x = \sqrt[9]{e}$

11) $x = \frac{e\, e^5}{11}$

12) $x = 42$

13) $x = 162$

14) 11

15) 10

16) 4

17) 21

18) 32

19) 20

20) 22

21) 27

22) 125

23) $\frac{1}{11}$

24) $\frac{1}{81}$

25) $\frac{64e^3}{125}$

26) 8

27) -4

28) 243

29) $\frac{13}{e}$

30) 0

31) 6

32) $\ln \left(\frac{1}{3^6 e^4}\right) = -10.6$

33) $25e^{-4} = \frac{25}{e^4}$

34) $\frac{4}{e}$

35) $11e$

Exponential Equations and Logarithms

1) $\frac{5}{4}$

2) $\frac{4}{3}$

3) 2

4) $-\frac{5}{4}$

5) $\frac{1}{4}$

6) $-\frac{5}{3}$

7) $\frac{7}{4}$

8) 4

Algebra 2

9) $\frac{3}{2}$
10) $\frac{3}{4}$
11) -1
12) -1
13) $\frac{1}{21}$
14) 1
15) $\frac{7}{5}$

16) 1
17) 3
18) $\frac{2}{3}$
19) $-\frac{3}{2}$
20) 2
21) 1
22) $\frac{7}{3}$

23) $-\frac{1}{2}$
24) 2
25) 3
26) 1
27) 24.2
28) 190.27
29) $\$12,432.4$
30) $\$10,792.14$

Solving Logarithmic Equations

1) $\{100\}$
2) $\{4\}$
3) $\{\frac{1}{64}\}$
4) $\{20\}$
5) $\{\frac{2}{25}\}$
6) $\{\frac{1}{250}\}$
7) $\{2\}$
8) $\{146\}$
9) $\{\frac{1}{4}\}$
10) No Solution
11) $\{\frac{1}{2}\}$
12) $\{-\frac{1}{3}\}$
13) $\{2\}$

14) No Solution
15) $\{1, -\frac{8}{5}\}$
16) $\{\frac{5}{7}\}$
17) $\{2, -2\}$
18) $\{1\}$
19) $x = \frac{8-8e^4}{4e^4}$
20) $\{-\frac{5}{3}\}$
21) $e^3 + 1$
22) $\{6\}$
23) $\{\frac{8}{3}\}$
24) $\{\frac{46}{17}\}$
25) $x = \frac{16e^5 - 2}{3}$

26) $x = \frac{9}{2}$
27) $x = \frac{11}{4}$
28) $x = \frac{20}{7}$
29) $e^{\frac{\ln(2)}{2}}$
30) No Solution
31) $x > 2$
32) No Solution
33) No Solution
34) $x = -\frac{3}{14}$
35) $x = \frac{5}{2}$
36) $x = \frac{5e+6}{5}$

Algebra 2

Chapter 11:
Conic Sections

Topics that you'll learn in this chapter:

- ✓ Equation of a Parabola
- ✓ Focus, Vertex, and Directrix of a Parabola
- ✓ Standard Form of a Circle
- ✓ Standard Equation of an Ellipse
- ✓ Hyperbola in Standard Form
- ✓ Conic Sections in Standard Form

He who takes nature for his guide, is not easily beaten out of his argument.
— *Thomas Paine*

Algebra 2

Equation of a Parabola

✎ **Write the equation of the following parabolas.**

1) Vertex (1, 2) and Focus (− 1, 2)

2) Vertex (3, 0) and Focus (2, 0)

3) Vertex (3, 2) and Focus (3, 0)

4) Vertex (1, 4) and Focus (1, 3)

5) Vertex (0, 5) and Focus (2, 5)

6) Vertex (4, 2) and Focus (4, 1)

7) Vertex (1, 3) and Focus (1, 6)

8) Vertex (5, 4) and Focus (8, 4)

9) Vertex (2, 1) and Focus (2, 8)

10) Vertex (3, 1) and Focus (0, 1)

Algebra 2

Focus, Vertex, and Directrix of a Parabola

✎ Use the information provided to write the vertex form equation of each parabola.

1) $y = x^2 + 4x - 6$

2) $y = x^2 - 10x + 22$

3) $y + 4 = x^2 + 8x$

4) $y = x^2 + 6x + 13$

5) $y - 41 = (x + 10)(x - 2)$

6) $\frac{1}{3}(y - 9) = (x - 6)^2$

7) $98x + 346 = -y - 7x^2$

8) $y = x^2 + 10x + 32$

9) Focus: $(-\frac{35}{2}, -5)$, Directrix: $x = -\frac{37}{2}$

10) Focus: $(\frac{97}{16}, 4)$, Directrix: $x = \frac{95}{16}$

11) Opens down or up, and passes through $(-2, -6), (-8, -6)$, and $(-5, 3)$

12) Opens down or up, and passes through $(4, 8), (5, 11)$, and $(2, 8)$

Algebra 2

Standard Form of a Circle

✎ **Write the standard form equation of each circle.**

1) $x^2 + y^2 - 10x - 4y + 28 = 0$

2) $y^2 + 6x + x^2 = 20y - 93$

3) $x^2 + y^2 - 6y + 10 = 10$

4) $16x + x^2 - 6y = -24 - y^2$

5) Center: $(-4, -5)$, Radius: 5

6) Center: $(-8, -14)$, Radius: 8

7) Center: $(-13, -7)$, Area: 9π

8) Center: $(-10, -15)$, Area: 36π

9) Center: $(-5, 4)$, Circumference: 4π

10) Center: $(12, 11)$, Circumference: $2\pi\sqrt{17}$

✎ **Identify the center and radius of each. Then sketch the graph.**

11) $(x - 3)^2 + (y + 4)^2 = 12$

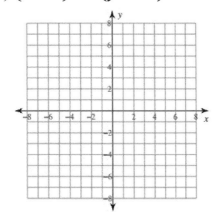

12) $(x - 2)^2 + y^2 = 9$

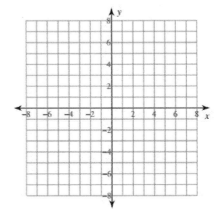

13) $(x - 1)^2 + (y + 4)^2 = 8$

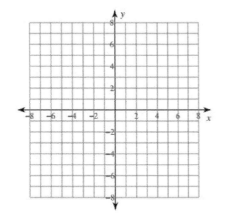

14) $(x + 12)^2 + (y - 4)^2 = 9$

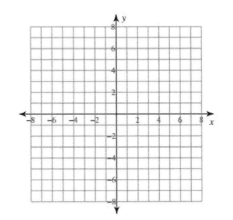

Algebra 2

Equation of Each Ellipse

✎ Use the information provided to write the standard form equation of each ellipse.

1) Foci: (4, 0), (–4, 0); Co–vertices: (0, 3), (0, –3)

2) Vertices: (0, 7), (0, –7); Co–vertices: (2, 0), (– 2, 0)

3) Vertices: (2, 3), (2, –9); Co–vertices: (6, – 3), (– 2, – 3)

4) Foci: (2√6, 0), (–2√6, 0); Co–vertices: (0, 5), (0, –5)

5) Foci: (–4, 3 + 2√5), (–4, 3 – 2√5); Co–vertices: (0, 3), (8, 3)

6) Vertices: (8, 2), (–2, 2); Co–vertices: (2, 6), (2, – 2)

7) Vertices: (11, 0), (–11, 0); Co–vertices: (0, 5), (0, –5)

8) Vertices: (19, –4), (– 7, –4); Co–vertices: (6, 5), (6, –13)

9) Center: (2, 6); Vertex: (2, 6 –√150); Co–vertex: (2 – √14, 6)

10) Center: (5, –12); Vertex: (17, –12); Co–vertex: (5, –20)

✎ Identify the vertices, co–vertices, foci.

11) $\dfrac{x^2}{225} + \dfrac{y^2}{81} = 1$

12) $\dfrac{x^2}{82} + \dfrac{y^2}{15} = 1$

13) $\dfrac{x^2}{64} + \dfrac{y^2}{25} = 1$

14) $\dfrac{x^2}{16} + \dfrac{y^2}{121} = 1$

15) $\dfrac{(x+4)^2}{36} + \dfrac{(y-2)^2}{100} = 1$

16) $\dfrac{(x-2)^2}{64} + \dfrac{(y-11)^2}{9} = 1$

17) $\dfrac{x^2}{49} + \dfrac{(y-9)^2}{4} = 1$

18) $\dfrac{x^2}{36} + \dfrac{(y-7)^2}{169} = 1$

WWW.MathNotion.Com

Algebra 2

Hyperbola in Standard Form

✎ **Use the information provided to write the standard form equation of each hyperbola.**

1) $-11x^2 + 14y^2 + 66x - 224y + 643 = 0$

2) $-x^2 + y^2 - 12x - 10y - 75 = 0$

3) $-4x^2 + y^2 + 24x + 4y - 48 = 0$

4) $x^2 - 9y^2 - 6x + 90y - 297 = 0$

5) Vertices: (5, 6), (–3, 6), Conjugate Axis is 8 units long

6) Vertices: (6, 1), (6, –23), Distance from Center to Focus = $4\sqrt{13}$

7) Vertices: (–7, 23), (–7, –7), Distance from Center to Focus = $5\sqrt{13}$

8) Vertices: (–3, –3), (–21, –3), Asymptotes: $y = x + 9$, $y = -x - 15$

9) Foci: (7, 2), (7, –10); Conjugate Axis is 12 units long

10) Foci: $(9, -3 + \sqrt{73})$, $(9, -3 - \sqrt{73})$, Endpoints of Conjugate Axis: (17, –3), (1, –3)

✎ **Identify the vertices, foci, and direction of opening of each.**

11) $\dfrac{y^2}{64} - \dfrac{x^2}{25} = 1$

12) $\dfrac{x^2}{169} - \dfrac{y^2}{64} = 1$

13) $\dfrac{x^2}{100} - \dfrac{y^2}{36} = 1$

14) $\dfrac{x^2}{49} - \dfrac{y^2}{16} = 1$

15) $\dfrac{(x+3)^2}{144} - \dfrac{(y+7)^2}{25} = 1$

16) $\dfrac{(y+9)^2}{81} - \dfrac{(x+4)^2}{64} =$

WWW.MathNotion.Com

Algebra 2

Conic Sections in Standard Form

✎ **Classify each conic section and write its equation in standard form.**

1) $x^2 + y^2 - 2x + 2y - 1 = 0$

2) $4x^2 - 16x + y^2 = 0$

3) $x^2 - y - 16x + 59 = 0$

4) $x^2 - 9y^2 - 54y - 90 = 0$

5) $x^2 - y^2 - 14x - 15 = 0$

6) $3x^2 - y + 12x + 7 = 0$

7) $y^2 + 16y + 4x^2 + 52 = 0$

8) $y^2 - x - 6y + 3 = 0$

✎ **Classify each conic section. (Not in Standard Form)**

9) $x^2 + y^2 - 6x + 6y - 9 = 0$

10) $x + 4y^2 - 30y + 84 = 0$

11) $x^2 - 2x + 2y^2 - 16y^2 + 16 = 0$

12) $x^2 - 25y^2 - 250y - 595 = 0$

13) $y^2 + 8x^2 - 80x + 75 = 0$

14) $x^2 + 4y^2 - x + 10y - 9 = 0$

15) $4x^2 + y^2 + 15y + 45 = 0$

16) $x^2 - 16x + y^2 + 16y - 48 = 0$

17) $2x^2 + 2y^2 + 25y - 25x + 60 = 0$

18) $x^2 + 4x - 9y^2 + 40y - 54 = 0$

19) $y = 8x^2 + 80x + 160$

20) $9x^2 + 16y^2 - 25y + 42x + 50 = 0$

21) $-x^2 - 49x + y^2 - 36y - 169 = 0$

22) $x^2 - 9y^2 - 16y + 48 = 0$

WWW.MathNotion.Com

Algebra 2

Answers of Worksheets

Equation of a Parabola

1) $(y-2)^2 = 8(1-x)$
2) $y^2 = 4(3-x)$
3) $(x-3)^2 = 8(2-y)$
4) $(x-1)^2 = 4(4-y)$
5) $(y-5)^2 = 8x$
6) $(x-4)^2 = 8-4y$
7) $(x-1)^2 = 12(y-3)$
8) $(y-4)^2 = 12(x-5)$
9) $(x-2)^2 = 28(y-1)$
10) $(y-1)^2 = 12(3-x)$

Focus, Vertex, and the Directrix of a Parabola

1) $y = (x+2)^2 - 10$
2) $y = (x-5)^2 - 3$
3) $y = (x+4)^2 - 20$
4) $y = (x+3)^2 + 4$
5) $y = (x+4)^2 + 5$
6) $y = 3(x-6)^2 + 9$
7) $y = -7(x+7)^2 - 3$
8) $y = (x+5)^2 + 7$
9) $x = \frac{1}{2}(y+5)^2 - 18$
10) $x = 4(y-4)^2 + 6$
11) $y = -(x+5)^2 + 3$
12) $y = (x-3)^2 + 7$

Standard Form of a Circle

1) $(x-5)^2 + (y-2)^2 = 1$
2) $(x+3)^2 + (y-10)^2 = 16$
3) $x^2 + (y-3)^2 = 9$
4) $(x+8)^2 + (y-3)^2 = 49$
5) $(x+4)^2 + (y+5)^2 = 25$
6) $(x+8)^2 + (y+14)^2 = 64$
7) $(x+13)^2 + (y+7)^2 = 9$
8) $(x+10)^2 + (y+15)^2 = 36$
9) $(x+5)^2 + (y-4)^2 = 4$
10) $(x-12)^2 + (y-11)^2 = 17$
11) Center: (3, –4), Radius: $\sqrt{12}$
12) Center: (2, 0), Radius: 3

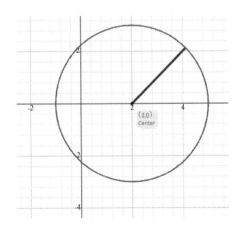

WWW.MathNotion.Com

Algebra 2

13) Center: (1, – 4), Radius: √8

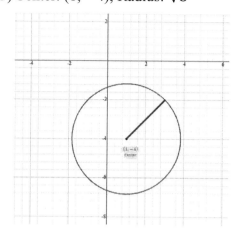

14) Center: (–12, 4), Radius: 3

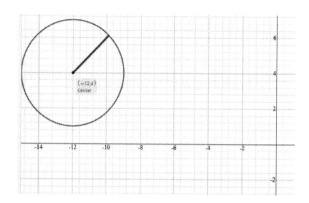

Equation of Each Ellipse

1) $\frac{x^2}{25} + \frac{y^2}{9} = 1$

2) $\frac{x^2}{4} + \frac{y^2}{49} = 1$

3) $\frac{(x-2)^2}{16} + \frac{(y+3)^2}{36} = 1$

4) $\frac{x^2}{49} + \frac{y^2}{25} = 1$

5) $\frac{(x+4)^2}{16} + \frac{(y-3)^2}{36} = 1$

6) $\frac{(x-3)^2}{25} + \frac{(y-2)^2}{16} = 1$

7) $\frac{x^2}{121} + \frac{y^2}{25} = 1$

8) $\frac{(x-6)^2}{169} + \frac{(y+4)^2}{9} = 1$

9) $\frac{(x-2)^2}{14} + \frac{(y-6)^2}{150} = 1$

10) $\frac{(x-5)^2}{144} + \frac{(y+12)^2}{64} = 1$

11) Vertices: (15, 0), (–15, 0); Co–vertices: (0, 9), (0, –9); Foci: (12, 0), (–12, 0)

12) Vertices: (√82, 0), (–√82, 0); Co–vertices: (0, √15), (0, –√15); Foci: (√67, 0), (–√67, 0)

13) Vertices: (8, 0), (–8, 0); Co–vertices: (0, 5), (0, –5); Foci: (√39, 0), (–√39, 0)

14) Vertices: (0, 11), (0, –11); Co–vertices: (4, 0), (–4, 0); Foci: (0, √105), (0, –√105)

15) Vertices: (–4, 12), (–4, –8); Co–vertices: (8, 2), (–4, 2); Foci: (–4, 10), (–4, –6)

16) Vertices: (10, 11), (–6, 11); Co–vertices: (2, 14), (2, 8); Foci: (2 + √55, 11), (2 – √55, 11)

17) Vertices: (7, 9), (–7, 9); Co–vertices: (0, 11), (0, 7); Foci: (3√5, 9), (–3√5, 9)

18) Vertices: (0, 20), (0, –6); Co–vertices: (6, 7), (–6, 7); Foci: (0, 7 + √133), (0, 7 – √133)

Hyperbola in Standard Form

1) $\frac{(y-8)^2}{11} - \frac{(x-3)^2}{14} = 1$

2) $\frac{(y-5)^2}{64} - \frac{(x+6)^2}{64} = 1$

3) $\frac{(y+2)^2}{16} - \frac{(x-3)^2}{4} = 1$

4) $\frac{(x-3)^2}{81} - \frac{(y-5)^2}{9} = 1$

Algebra 2

5) $\dfrac{(x-1)^2}{16} - \dfrac{(y-6)^2}{121} = 1$

6) $\dfrac{(y+11)^2}{144} - \dfrac{(x-6)^2}{64} = 1$

7) $\dfrac{(y-8)^2}{225} - \dfrac{(x+7)^2}{100} = 1$

8) $\dfrac{(x+12)^2}{81} - \dfrac{(y+3)^2}{81} = 1$

9) $\dfrac{(y+4)^2}{36} - \dfrac{(x-7)^2}{36} = 1$

10) $\dfrac{(y+3)^2}{9} - \dfrac{(x-9)^2}{64} = 1$

11) Vertices: (0, 8), (0, –8); Foci: (0, $\sqrt{89}$), (0, – $\sqrt{89}$); Opens up/down

12) Vertices: (13, 0), (–13, 0); Foci: ($\sqrt{233}$, 0), (–$\sqrt{233}$, 0); Opens left/right

13) Vertices: (10, 0), (–10, 0); Foci: ($2\sqrt{34}$, 0), (–$2\sqrt{34}$, 0); Opens left/right

14) Vertices: (7, 0), (–7, 0); Foci: ($\sqrt{65}$, 0), (–$\sqrt{65}$, 0); Opens left/right

15) Vertices: (9, –7), (–15, –7); Foci: (10, –7), (–16, –7); Opens left/right

16) Vertices: (–4, 0), (–4, –18); Foci: (–4, –9 + $\sqrt{145}$), (–4, –9 – $\sqrt{154}$); Opens up/down

Conic Sections in Standard Form

1) Circle, $(x-1)^2 + (y+1)^2 = 3$

2) Ellipse, $\dfrac{(x-2)^2}{4} + \dfrac{y^2}{16} = 1$

3) Parabola, $y = (x-8)^2 - 5$

4) Hyperbola, $\dfrac{x^2}{9} - (y+3)^2 = 1$

5) Hyperbola, $\dfrac{(x-7)^2}{64} - \dfrac{y^2}{64} = 1$

6) Parabola, $y = 3(x+2)^2 - 5$

7) Ellipse, $4x^2 + (y+8)^2 = 12$

8) Parabola, $x = (y-3)^2 - 6$

9) Circle

10) Parabola

11) Hyperbola

12) Hyperbola

13) Ellipse

14) Ellipse

15) Ellipse

16) Circle

17) Circle

18) Hyperbola

19) Parabola

20) Ellipse

21) Hyperbola

22) Hyperbola

Algebra 2

Chapter 12:
Trigonometric Functions

Topics that you'll practice in this chapter:

- ✓ Trig ratios of General Angles
- ✓ Sketch Each Angle in Standard Position
- ✓ Finding Co–Terminal Angles and Reference Angles
- ✓ Angles in Radians
- ✓ Angles in Degrees
- ✓ Evaluating Each Trigonometric Expression
- ✓ Missing Sides and Angles of a Right Triangle
- ✓ Arc Length and Sector Area

Mathematics is like checkers in being suitable for the young, not too difficult, amusing, and without peril to the state. — Plato

Algebra 2

Trig ratios of General Angles

✎ **Evaluate.**

1) $\sin 135° = $ _____

2) $\sin 300° = $ _____

3) $\cos -225° = $ _____

4) $\cos 270° = $ _____

5) $\sin 450° = $ _____

6) $\sin -330° = $ _____

7) $\tan 60° = $ _____

8) $\cot 180° = $ _____

9) $\tan 240° = $ _____

10) $\cot 90° = $ _____

11) $\sec 180° = $ _____

12) $\csc 90° = $ _____

13) $\cot -270° = $ _____

14) $\sec 360° = $ _____

15) $\cos -45° = $ _____

16) $\sec 120° = $ _____

17) $\csc 360° = $ _____

18) $\cot -45° = $ _____

✎ **Find the exact value of each trigonometric function. Some may be undefined.**

19) $\sec 2\pi = $ _____

20) $\tan -\dfrac{5\pi}{2} = $ _____

21) $\cos \dfrac{11\pi}{2} = $ _____

22) $\cot \dfrac{9\pi}{4} = $ _____

23) $\sec -6\pi = $ _____

24) $\sec \dfrac{\pi}{4} = $ _____

25) $\csc \dfrac{8\pi}{3} = $ _____

26) $\cot \dfrac{10\pi}{3} = $ _____

27) $\csc -\dfrac{\pi}{2} = $ _____

28) $\cot \dfrac{2\pi}{3} = $ _____

Algebra 2

Sketch Each Angle in Standard Position

✎ **Draw each angle with the given measure in standard position.**

1) −570°

4) −690°

2) 750°

5) $\frac{13\pi}{6}$

3) 1,110°

6) $-\frac{11\pi}{6}$

Algebra 2

Finding Co-terminal Angles and Reference Angles

✎ **Find a conterminal angle between 0° and 360° for each angle provided.**

1) $-315° =$

3) $-225° =$

2) $-210° =$

4) $-540° =$

✎ **Find a conterminal angle between 0 and 2π for each given angle.**

5) $\dfrac{18\pi}{5} =$

7) $-\dfrac{13\pi}{4} =$

6) $-\dfrac{19\pi}{6} =$

8) $\dfrac{14\pi}{3} =$

✎ **Find the reference angle of each angle.**

9)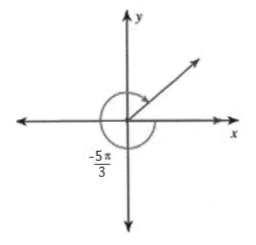

10)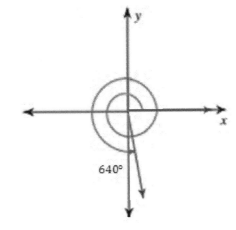

Algebra 2

Angles and Angle Measure

✎ **Convert each degree measure into radians.**

1) $216° = $ ____

2) $660° = $ ____

3) $420° = $ ____

4) $220° = $ ____

5) $210° = $ ____

6) $270° = $ ____

7) $-300° = $ ____

8) $810° = $ ____

9) $330° = $ ____

10) $140° = $ ____

11) $480° = $ ____

12) $405° = $ ____

13) $-450° = $ ____

14) $-126° = $ ____

15) $-675° = $ ____

16) $150° = $ ____

17) $-468° = $ ____

18) $340° = $ ____

19) $-440° = $ ____

20) $342° = $ ____

21) $230° = $ ____

✎ **Convert each radian measure into degrees.**

22) $\frac{\pi}{10} =$

23) $\frac{5\pi}{12} =$

24) $\frac{7\pi}{3} =$

25) $\frac{3\pi}{20} =$

26) $-\frac{6\pi}{5} =$

27) $\frac{11\pi}{18} =$

28) $-\frac{14\pi}{5} =$

29) $\frac{5\pi}{18} =$

30) $\frac{7\pi}{36} =$

31) $\frac{17\pi}{18} =$

32) $-\frac{13\pi}{30} =$

33) $\frac{7\pi}{9} =$

34) $-\frac{19\pi}{18} =$

35) $\frac{7\pi}{60} =$

36) $-\frac{3\pi}{10} =$

37) $\frac{11\pi}{30} =$

38) $-\frac{2\pi}{9} =$

39) $-\frac{7\pi}{10} =$

WWW.MathNotion.Com

Algebra 2

Evaluating Trigonometric Functions

✎ **Find the exact value of each trigonometric function.**

1) $\cos 780° = $ _____

2) $\tan \dfrac{5\pi}{3} = $ _____

3) $\tan -\dfrac{\pi}{6} = $ _____

4) $\cot -\dfrac{9\pi}{4} = $ _____

5) $\cos -\dfrac{7\pi}{6} = $ _____

6) $\cos 135° = $ _____

7) $\sin 240° = $ _____

8) $\tan 330° = $ _____

9) $\cot 420° = $ _____

10) $\tan -495° = $ _____

11) $\cot 315° = $ _____

12) $\sin -240° = $ _____

13) $\cot 225° = $ _____

✎ **Use the given point on the terminal side of angle θ to find the value of the trigonometric function indicated.**

14) $\sin \theta;\ (-6, 8)$

15) $\cos \theta;\ (-6, 8)$

16) $\sec \theta;\ (3, 5)$

17) $\cos \theta;\ (10, 24)$

18) $\sin \theta;\ (6, -6)$

19) $\tan \theta;\ (-2, -\sqrt{12})$

Algebra 2

Missing Sides and Angles of a Right Triangle

✎ Find the value of each trigonometric ratio as fractions in their simplest form.

1) cot x

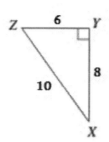

2) cos A

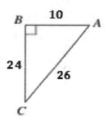

✎ Find the missing sides. Round answers to the nearest tenth.

3)

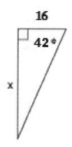

4)

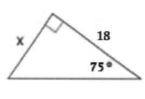

5)

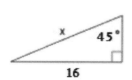

6)

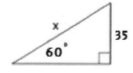

WWW.MathNotion.Com

Algebra 2

Arc Length and Sector Area

✎ **Find the length of each arc. Round your answers to the nearest tenth.**

($\pi = 3.14$)

1) $r = 28$ cm, $\theta = 30°$

3) $r = 22$ ft, $\theta = 50°$

2) $r = 14$ ft, $\theta = 95°$

4) $r = 16$ m, $\theta = 85°$

✎ **Find area of each sector. Do *not* round. Round your answers to the nearest tenth.** ($\pi = 3.14$)

5)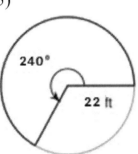

7)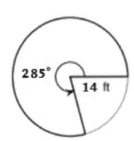

6)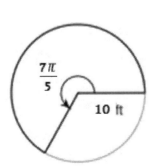

8)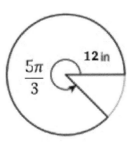

Algebra 2

Answers of Worksheets

Trig Ratios of General Angles

1) $\frac{\sqrt{2}}{2}$

2) $-\frac{\sqrt{3}}{2}$

3) $-\frac{\sqrt{2}}{2}$

4) 0

5) 1

6) $\frac{1}{2}$

7) $\sqrt{3}$

8) Undefined

9) $\sqrt{3}$

10) 0

11) -1

12) 1

13) 0

14) 1

15) $\frac{\sqrt{2}}{2}$

16) -2

17) Undefined

18) -1

19) 1

20) Undefined

21) 0

22) 1

23) 1

24) $\sqrt{2}$

25) $\frac{2\sqrt{3}}{3}$

26) $\frac{\sqrt{3}}{3}$

27) -1

28) $-\frac{\sqrt{3}}{3}$

Sketch Each Angle in Standard Position

1) $-570°$

2) $750°$

3) $1,110°$

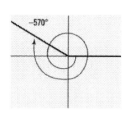 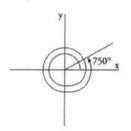 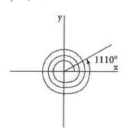

4) $-690°$

5) $\frac{13\pi}{6} = 390°$

6) $-\frac{11\pi}{6} = -330°$

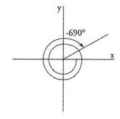 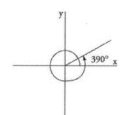 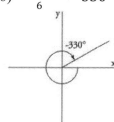

Finding Co–Terminal Angles and Reference Angles

1) $45°$

2) $150°$

3) $135°$

4) $180°$

5) $\frac{4\pi}{5}$

6) $\frac{5\pi}{6}$

7) $\frac{3\pi}{4}$

8) $\frac{2\pi}{3}$

9) $\frac{\pi}{3}$

10) $80°$

Angles and Angle Measure

Algebra 2

1) $\frac{6\pi}{5}$
2) $\frac{11\pi}{3}$
3) $\frac{7\pi}{3}$
4) $\frac{11\pi}{9}$
5) $\frac{7\pi}{6}$
6) $\frac{3\pi}{2}$
7) $-\frac{5\pi}{3}$
8) $\frac{9\pi}{2}$
9) $\frac{11\pi}{6}$
10) $\frac{7\pi}{9}$
11) $\frac{8\pi}{3}$
12) $\frac{9\pi}{4}$
13) $-\frac{5}{2}\pi$
14) $-\frac{7\pi}{10}$
15) $-\frac{15\pi}{4}$
16) $\frac{5\pi}{6}$
17) $-\frac{13\pi}{5}$
18) $\frac{17\pi}{9}$
19) $-\frac{22\pi}{9}$
20) $\frac{19\pi}{10}$
21) $\frac{23\pi}{18}$
22) $18°$
23) $75°$
24) $420°$
25) $27°$
26) $-216°$
27) $110°$
28) $-504°$
29) $50°$
30) $35°$
31) $170°$
32) $-78°$
33) $140°$
34) $-190°$
35) $21°$
36) $-54°$
37) $66°$
38) $-40°$
39) $-126°$

Evaluating Each Trigonometric Functions

1) $\frac{1}{2}$
2) $-\sqrt{3}$
3) $-\frac{\sqrt{3}}{3}$
4) -1
5) $-\frac{\sqrt{3}}{2}$
6) $-\frac{\sqrt{2}}{2}$
7) $-\frac{\sqrt{3}}{2}$
8) $-\frac{\sqrt{3}}{3}$
9) $\frac{\sqrt{3}}{3}$
10) 1
11) -1
12) $\frac{\sqrt{3}}{2}$
13) 1
14) 0.8
15) -0.6
16) $\frac{\sqrt{34}}{5}$
17) $\frac{5}{13}$
18) $-\frac{\sqrt{2}}{2}$
19) $\sqrt{3}$

Missing Sides and Angles of a Right Triangle

1) $\frac{4}{3}$
2) $\frac{5}{13}$
3) 14.4
4) 67.2
5) 22.6
6) 40.4

Arc Length and Sector Area

1) $14.7\ cm$
2) $23.2\ ft$
3) $19.2\ ft$
4) $23.7 m$
5) $1,013.7\ ft^2$
6) $220\ in^2$
7) $487.5\ ft^2$
8) $377\ in^2$

Algebra 2

Chapter 13 :
Statistics and Probability

Topics that you'll practice in this chapter:

- ✓ Probability Problems
- ✓ Factorials
- ✓ Combinations and Permutation

Mathematics is no more computation than typing is literature.

− John Allen Paulos

Algebra 2

Probability Problems

✏ **Calculate.**

1) A number is chosen at random from 1 to 10. Find the probability of selecting number 6 or smaller numbers. _____

2) Bag A contains 18 red marbles and 6 green marbles. Bag B contains 16 black marbles and 8 orange marbles. What is the probability of selecting a green marble at random from bag A? What is the probability of selecting a black marble at random from Bag B? _____

3) A number is chosen at random from 1 to 20. What is the probability of selecting multiples of 4? _____

4) A card is chosen from a well-shuffled deck of 52 cards. What is the probability that the card will be a queen? _____

5) A number is chosen at random from 1 to 15. What is the probability of selecting a multiple of 3 or 5? _____

A spinner numbered 1–8, is spun once. What is the probability of spinning …?

6) an Odd number? _____   7) a multiple of 2? _____

8) a multiple of 5? _____   9) number 10? _____

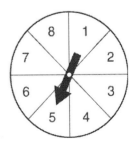

Algebra 2

Factorials

✎ **Determine the value for each expression.**

1) $4! + 0! =$

2) $2! + 5! =$

3) $(2!)^2 =$

4) $5! - 3! =$

5) $6! - 3! + 10 =$

6) $3! \times 4 - 15 =$

7) $(2! + 3!)^2 =$

8) $(4! - 3!)^2 =$

9) $(3!\,0!)^2 - 10 =$

10) $\dfrac{10!}{8!} =$

11) $\dfrac{6!}{4!} =$

12) $\dfrac{6!}{5!} =$

13) $\dfrac{15!}{13!} =$

14) $\dfrac{n!}{(n-3)!} =$

15) $\dfrac{(n+2)!}{n!} =$

16) $\dfrac{(2+2!)^3}{2!} =$

17) $\dfrac{5(n+2)!}{(n+1)!} =$

18) $\dfrac{22!}{20!4!} =$

19) $\dfrac{13!}{11!3!} =$

20) $\dfrac{9 \times 210!}{3(7 \times 30)!} =$

21) $\dfrac{32!}{31!2!} =$

22) $\dfrac{11!12!}{10!13!} =$

23) $\dfrac{16!15!}{14!14!} =$

24) $\dfrac{(5 \times 3)!}{0!14!} =$

25) $\dfrac{4!(5n-2)!}{(5n)!} =$

26) $\dfrac{4n(4n+7)!}{(4n+8)!} =$

27) $\dfrac{(n-2)!(n+1)}{(n+2)!} =$

Algebra 2

Combinations and Permutations

✎ **Calculate the value of each.**

1) $6! =$ ____

2) $2! \times 5! =$ ____

3) $3 \times 4! =$ ____

4) $5! + 3! =$ ____

5) $7! =$ ____

6) $4! =$ ____

7) $3! + 3! =$ ____

8) $7! - 5! =$ ____

✎ **Find the answer for each word problems.**

9) Susan is baking cookies. She uses sugar, butter, Vanilla, eggs and flour. How many different orders of ingredients can she try? _____

10) Albert is planning for his vacation. He wants to go to museum, watch a movie, go to the beach, play the game and play football. How many ways of ordering are there for him? _____

11) How many 4-digit numbers can be named using the digits 3, 4, 5, and 6 without repetition? _____

12) In how many ways can 5 boys be arranged in a straight line? _____

13) In how many ways can 6 athletes be arranged in a straight line? _____

14) A professor is going to arrange her 7 students in a straight line. In how many ways can she do this? _____

15) How many code symbols can be formed with the letters for the word GAMES? _____

16) In how many ways a team of 7 basketball players can choose a captain and co-captain? _____

Algebra 2

Answers of Worksheets

Probability Problems

1) $\frac{3}{5}$
2) $\frac{1}{4}, \frac{2}{3}$
3) $\frac{1}{4}$
4) $\frac{1}{13}$
5) $\frac{7}{15}$
6) $\frac{1}{2}$
7) $\frac{1}{2}$
8) $\frac{1}{8}$
9) 0

Factorials

1) 25
2) 122
3) 4
4) 114
5) 724
6) 9
7) 64
8) 324
9) 26
10) 90
11) 30
12) 6
13) 210
14) $n(n-1)(n-2)$
15) $(n+1)(n+2)$
16) 32
17) $5(n+2)$
18) 19.25
19) 26
20) 3
21) 16
22) $\frac{11}{13}$
23) 3,600
24) 15
25) $\frac{24}{5n(5n-1)}$
26) $\frac{n}{(n+2)}$
27) $\frac{1}{n(n-1)(n+2)}$

Combinations and Permutations

1) 720
2) 240
3) 72
4) 126
5) 5,040
6) 24
7) 12
8) 4,920
9) 120
10) 120
11) 24
12) 120
13) 720
14) 5,040
15) 120
16) 42

WWW.MathNotion.Com

Algebra 2

Algebra 2

Chapter 14:
Algebra 2 Practice Tests

Time to Test

Time to refine your skill with a practice examination.

Take a REAL Algebra 2 test to simulate the test day experience. After you've finished, score your test using the answer key.

Before You Start

- You'll need a pencil, calculator, and a timer to take the test.
- It's okay to guess. You won't lose any points if you're wrong.
- After you've finished the test, review the answer key to see where you went wrong.

Graphing calculators are Not permitted for Algebra 2 Tests.

Good Luck!

Algebra 2

Algebra 2

Algebra Practice Tests Answer Sheet

Remove (photocopy) this answer sheet and use it to complete the practice test.

Algebra 2 Practice Test Answer Sheet

1 Ⓐ Ⓑ Ⓒ Ⓓ	11 Ⓐ Ⓑ Ⓒ Ⓓ	21 Ⓐ Ⓑ Ⓒ Ⓓ
2 Ⓐ Ⓑ Ⓒ Ⓓ	12 Ⓐ Ⓑ Ⓒ Ⓓ	22 Ⓐ Ⓑ Ⓒ Ⓓ
3 Ⓐ Ⓑ Ⓒ Ⓓ	13 Ⓐ Ⓑ Ⓒ Ⓓ	23 Ⓐ Ⓑ Ⓒ Ⓓ
4 Ⓐ Ⓑ Ⓒ Ⓓ	14 Ⓐ Ⓑ Ⓒ Ⓓ	24 Ⓐ Ⓑ Ⓒ Ⓓ
5 Ⓐ Ⓑ Ⓒ Ⓓ	15 Ⓐ Ⓑ Ⓒ Ⓓ	25 Ⓐ Ⓑ Ⓒ Ⓓ
6 Ⓐ Ⓑ Ⓒ Ⓓ	16 Ⓐ Ⓑ Ⓒ Ⓓ	26 Ⓐ Ⓑ Ⓒ Ⓓ
7 Ⓐ Ⓑ Ⓒ Ⓓ	17 Ⓐ Ⓑ Ⓒ Ⓓ	27 Ⓐ Ⓑ Ⓒ Ⓓ
8 Ⓐ Ⓑ Ⓒ Ⓓ	18 Ⓐ Ⓑ Ⓒ Ⓓ	28 Ⓐ Ⓑ Ⓒ Ⓓ
9 Ⓐ Ⓑ Ⓒ Ⓓ	19 Ⓐ Ⓑ Ⓒ Ⓓ	29 Ⓐ Ⓑ Ⓒ Ⓓ
10 Ⓐ Ⓑ Ⓒ Ⓓ	20 Ⓐ Ⓑ Ⓒ Ⓓ	30 Ⓐ Ⓑ Ⓒ Ⓓ

Algebra 2

Algebra 2

Algebra 2 Practice Test 1

✓ 30 Questions

✓ You may use a calculator for this test.

Released *Month Year*

Algebra 2

1) If $\frac{7x}{64} = \frac{x-3}{8}$, $x = ?$

   A. $\frac{1}{24}$

   B. $\frac{1}{18}$

   C. 18

   D. 24

2) Three years ago, Amy was four times as old as Mike was. If Mike is 7 years old now, how old is Amy?

   A. 19

   B. 18

   C. 14

   D. 11

3) If $y = 3ab + 4b^2$, what is y when $a = 5$ and $b = 3$?

   A. 45

   B. 81

   C. 36

   D. 48

4) If $f(x) = 4 + 5x$ and $g(x) = -3x^2 - 8 - x$, then find $(g - f)(x)$?

   A. $3x^2 - 6x - 12$

   B. $3x^2 - 6x + 12$

   C. $-3x^2 - 6x + 12$

   D. $-3x^2 - 6x - 12$

5) What is the area of a square whose diagonal is 10 cm?

   A. 25 cm²

   B. 50 cm²

   C. 75 cm²

   D. 100 cm²

6) If $(x - 6)^3 = 8$ which of the following could be the value of $(x - 3)(x - 2)$?

   A. 8

   B. 30

   C. −12

   D. −14

Algebra 2

7) What is the value of x in the following figure?

   A. 156

   B. 163

   C. 62

   D. 115

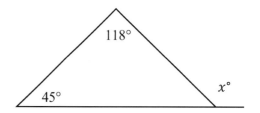

8) Right triangle ABC is shown below. Which of the following is true for all possible values of angle A and B?

   A. $\cos A = \tan B$

   B. $\tan^2 A = \tan^2 B$

   C. $\cot A = \cos B$

   D. $\cos A = \sin B$

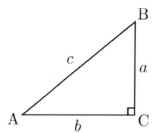

9) From the figure, which of the following must be true? (figure not drawn to scale)

   A. $y = 6x$

   B. $3y \geq x$

   C. $3y + 6x = z$

   D. $z > 3x$

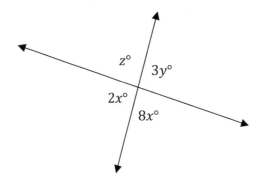

10) From last year, the price of gasoline has increased from $1.95 per gallon to $2.34 per gallon. The new price is what percent of the original price?

   A. 80%   C. 110%

   B. 120%   D. 140%

Algebra 2

11) What is the value of x in the following system of equations?

$$x + 3y = 6$$
$$3x + 7y = 14$$

A. 0

B. 1

C. – 1

D. 3

12) Simplify.

$$5x^4 + 6y^6 - 3x^4 + 7z^3 - y^4 + 3x^3 - 4y^6 + 5z^3$$

A. $2x^4 + 2y^6 - y^4 + 12z^3$

B. $2x^4 + 3x^3 - 2y^6 + 12z^3$

C. $2x^4 + 3x^3 + 2y^6 - y^4 + 12z^3$

D. $2x^4 - 3x^3 + 2y^6 - y^4 + 5z^3$

13) A ladder leans against a wall forming a 60° angle between the ground and the ladder. If the bottom of the ladder is 20 feet away from the wall, how long is the ladder?

A. 10 feet

B. 30 feet

C. 20 feet

D. 40 feet

14) The length of a rectangle is 6 meters greater than 4 times its width. The perimeter of the rectangle is 42 meters. What is the area of the rectangle?

A. 21 m²

B. 84 m²

C. 54 m²

D. 52 m²

Algebra 2

15) Simplify $(-3 + 4i)(7 + 5i)$,

    A. $41 - 11i$ C. $-13 + 41i$

    B. $11 - 41i$ D. $-41 + 13i$

16) If $tan\ \theta = \frac{3}{4}$ and $sin\ \theta > 0$, then $sin\ \theta =$?

    A. $-\frac{4}{5}$ C. $\frac{5}{3}$

    B. $\frac{3}{5}$ D. $-\frac{5}{4}$

17) Which of the following has the one fourth period and three times the amplitude of graph $y = sinx$?

    A. $y = \frac{1}{3} sin\ 4x$ C. $y = 3 + 3\ sin\ 4x$

    B. $y = 4sin\ (\frac{x}{3} + 4)$ D. $y = 3 + sin\ \frac{x}{4}$

18) y is $x\%$ of what number?

    A. $\frac{y}{10x}$ C. $\frac{100y}{x}$

    B. $\frac{10x}{y}$ D. $\frac{10x}{y}$

19) What is the solution of the following inequality?

$$|x - 7| \leq 3$$

    A. $x \geq 10 \cup x \leq 4$ C. $x \geq 11$

    B. $4 \leq x \leq 10$ D. $x \leq 4$

Algebra 2

20) If cotangent of an angel β is $\sqrt{3}$, then the tangent of angle β is

   A. $\frac{\sqrt{3}}{3}$

   B. $-\frac{\sqrt{3}}{3}$

   C. 1

   D. 0

21) Which of the following points lies on the line $3x - 4y = 13$?

   A. $(4, -1)$

   B. $(-2, 2)$

   C. $(-1, -4)$

   D. $(-1, -3)$

22) In the xy-plane, the point $(5, 7)$ and $(4, 6)$ are on the line A. Which of the following equations of lines is parallel to line A?

   A. $y = 3x$

   B. $y = \frac{x}{2}$

   C. $y = -2x$

   D. $y = x$

23) When point A $(5, 1)$ is reflected over the y-axis to get the point B, what are the coordinates of point B?

   A. $(5, 1)$

   B. $(-5, -1)$

   C. $(-5, 1)$

   D. $(5, -1)$

24) A bag contains 15 balls: two green, five black, three blue, a brown, three red and one white. If 10 balls are removed from the bag at random, what is the probability that a brown ball has been removed?

   A. $\frac{2}{3}$

   B. $\frac{1}{5}$

   C. $\frac{1}{10}$

   D. $\frac{1}{15}$

Algebra 2

25) If 70% of x equal to 20% of 35, then what is the value of $(x + 4)^2$?

   A. 19.96

   B. 14.14

   C. 2,096

   D. 196

26) If $f(x) = x^4 + 2x^3 + 3x$ and $g(x) = -3$, what is the value of $f(g(x))$?

   A. 9

   B. 0

   C. 12

   D. 18

27) If $x \begin{bmatrix} 4 & 0 \\ 0 & 3 \end{bmatrix} = \begin{bmatrix} 3x + y - 7 & 0 \\ 0 & 2y - 13 \end{bmatrix}$, what is the product of x and y?

   A. 6

   B. 11

   C. 8

   D. 1

28) If $f(x) = 3^x$ and $g(x) = log_3 x$, which of the following expressions is equal to $f(3g(p))$?

   A. $3P$

   B. 3^p

   C. p^3

   D. $\frac{p}{3}$

29) If one angle of a right triangle measures 30°, what is the sine of the other acute angle?

   A. $\frac{\sqrt{3}}{2}$

   B. $\frac{\sqrt{2}}{2}$

   C. $\frac{1}{2}$

   D. $\sqrt{2}$

Algebra 2

30) In the following equation when z is divided by 4, what is the effect on x?

$$x = \frac{5y + \frac{r}{4r+7}}{\frac{10}{z}}$$

A. x is divided by 8.

B. x is divided by 4.

C. x is multiplied by 4.

D. x is multiplied by 8.

STOP

This is the End of this Test. You may check your work on this Test if you still have time.

Algebra 2

Algebra 2
Practice Test 2

✓ **30 Questions**

✓ **You may use a calculator for this test.**

Released *Month Year*

Algebra 2

1) A number is chosen at random from 1 to 20. Find the probability of not selecting a composite number.

   A. $\frac{7}{20}$

   B. 12

   C. $\frac{2}{5}$

   D. 0.5

2) Simplify $\frac{10-2i}{-5i}$?

   A. $\frac{2}{5} + 2i$

   B. $\frac{7}{5} - 2i$

   C. $\frac{4}{5} - i$

   D. $\frac{3}{5} + i$

3) If $\sqrt{9x} = \sqrt{y}$, then $x =$?

   A. $\sqrt{\frac{y}{9}}$

   B. $9y^2$

   C. $\sqrt{9y}$

   D. $\frac{y}{9}$

4) If $f(x) = 7x - 2$ and $g(x) = 4x^2 - 3x$, then find $\left(\frac{f}{g}\right)(x)$.

   A. $\frac{7x-2}{4x^2-3x}$

   B. $\frac{2x-7}{4x^2-3x}$

   C. $\frac{7x-4}{x^2-3}$

   D. $\frac{7x+2}{4x^2+3x}$

5) In the standard (x, y) coordinate plane, which of the following lines contains the points $(2, -4)$ and $(4, 6)$?

   A. $y = 5x - 14$

   B. $y = -5x + 14$

   C. $y = -\frac{1}{5}x + 7$

   D. $y = 5x - 7$

Algebra 2

6) If the interior angles of a quadrilateral are in the ratio 2:5:6:11, what is the measure of the largest angle?

    A. 175°   C. 115°

    B. 30°   D. 165°

7) If $x + 3sin^2 a + 3cos^2 a = 9$, then $x = ?$

    A. 3   C. 12

    B. 6   D. 9

8) An angle is equal to one ninth of its supplement. What is the measure of that angle?

    A. 18   C. 45

    B. 15.5   D. 90

9) If $cos\alpha = \frac{\sqrt{5}}{3}$ in a right triangle and the angle α is an acute angle, then what is $cos\ \alpha$?

    A. $\frac{\sqrt{3}}{5}$ C. $\sqrt{5}$

    B. $\frac{1}{5}$ D. $\frac{2}{3}$

10) What are the zeroes of the function $f(x) = 3x^3 + 30x^2 + 63x$?

    A. $-1, 3$ C. $0, -3, -7$

    B. $0, 3, 7$ D. $-7, -1$

Algebra 2

11) In the standard (x, y) coordinate system plane, what is the area of the circle with the following equation?

$$(x+3)^2 + (y-5)^2 = 4$$

A. 2π

B. 4π

C. 16π

D. 8π

12) Simplify.

$$7x^6y^3 + 3x^2y^7 - (4x^6y^3 - 8x^2y^7)$$

A. $-x^6y^3$

B. $11x^6y^3 - 3x^2y^7$

C. $3x^6y^7$

D. $3x^6y^3 + 11x^2y^7$

13) In the following figure, what is the perimeter of $\triangle ABC$ if the area of $\triangle ADC$ is 35?

A. 28.5

B. 70

C. 35

D. 60

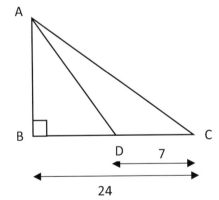

14) Which of the following is one solution of this equation?

$$8x^2 + 7x - 1 = 0$$

A. $\sqrt{7} + 1$

B. $\sqrt{7} - 1$

C. -1

D. $\sqrt{14}$

Algebra 2

15) Two-kilograms apple and five-kilograms orange cost $48.8. If one-kilogram apple costs $1.9 how much does one-kilogram orange cost?

   A. $9

   B. $7

   C. $12.5

   D. $8.5

16) Which of the following expressions is equal to $\sqrt{\dfrac{5x^2}{7} + \dfrac{x^2}{49}}$?

   A. $7x$

   B. $\dfrac{6x}{7}$

   C. $13x\sqrt{x}$

   D. $\dfrac{x\sqrt{x}}{6}$

17) Tickets to a movie cost $13.50 for adults and $4.50 for students. A group of 16 friends purchased tickets for $108. How many student tickets did they buy?

   A. 6

   B. 12

   C. 10

   D. 20

18) If $x = 5$, what is the value of y in the following equation? $7y = \dfrac{4x^2}{5} + 8$

   A. 4

   B. 12

   C. 25

   D. 10

19) Let r and p be constants. If $x^2 + 8x + r$ factors into $(x + 6)(x + p)$, the values of r and p respectively are?

   A. 12, 2

   B. 2, 10

   C. 4, 12

   D. 10, 2

Algebra 2

20) If 160% of a number is 80, then what is 60% of that number?

   A. 45

   B. 65

   C. 30

   D. 50

21) The average of four consecutive numbers is 28. What is the smallest number?

   A. 29

   B. 27.5

   C. 26.5

   D. 25.5

22) In a coordinate plane, triangle ABC has coordinates: $(7, -2)$, $(-3, -5)$, and $(4, 7)$. If triangle ABC is reflected over the y-axis, what are the coordinates of the new image?

   A. $(-7, 2), (3, 5), (-4, -7)$

   B. $(7, 2), (-3, 5), (4, -7)$

   C. $(-7, -2), (3, -5), (-4, 7)$

   D. $(7, -2), (-3, 5), (4, -7)$

23) What is the slope of a line that is perpendicular to the line $9x - 3y = 18$?

   A. -3

   B. $-\frac{1}{3}$

   C. 1

   D. 9

24) If $f(x) = 2x^4 + 7$ and $g(x) = \frac{1}{x}$, what is the value of $f(g(x))$?

   A. $\frac{7}{2x^4 + 1}$

   B. $\frac{7}{x^4}$

   C. $\frac{1}{2x + 7}$

   D. $\frac{2}{x^4} + 7$

Algebra 2

25) What is the solution of the following inequality?

$$|x - 5| \geq 9$$

A. $x \geq 14 \cup x \leq -4$

B. $-4 \leq x \leq 14$

C. $x \geq 14$

D. $x \leq -4$

26) If $\tan x = \frac{21}{28}$, then $\cos x =$

A. $\frac{1}{4}$

B. $\frac{4}{5}$

C. $\frac{21}{35}$

D. $\frac{5}{7}$

27) In the following figure, ABCD is a rectangle. If $a = \sqrt{3}$, and $b = 4a$, find the area of the shaded region. (the shaded region is a trapezoid)

A. 10

B. $8\sqrt{3}$

C. $10\sqrt{3}$

D. $12\sqrt{3}$

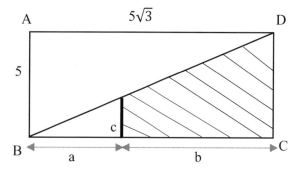

28) If the ratio of $7a$ to $6b$ is $\frac{1}{18}$, what is the ratio of a to b?

A. 20

B. $\frac{1}{21}$

C. $\frac{7}{18}$

D. $\frac{1}{26}$

Algebra 2

29) If $A = \begin{bmatrix} 2 & 2 \\ 4 & -2 \end{bmatrix}$ and $B = \begin{bmatrix} -5 & 3 \\ -4 & 6 \end{bmatrix}$, then $2A + B =$

A. $\begin{bmatrix} -1 & 4 \\ 7 & -2 \end{bmatrix}$

B. $\begin{bmatrix} -1 & 7 \\ 4 & -2 \end{bmatrix}$

C. $\begin{bmatrix} 1 & 3 \\ -4 & 7 \end{bmatrix}$

D. $\begin{bmatrix} -1 & 7 \\ 4 & 2 \end{bmatrix}$

30) What is the amplitude of the graph of the equation $y - 4 = 7cos4x$? (half the distance between the graph's minimum and maximum y-values in standard (x, y) coordinate plane is the amplitude of a graph.)

A. 4

B. 7

C. 8

D. 3

STOP

This is the End of this Test. You may check your work on this Test if you still have time.

Algebra 2

Chapter 15 :
Answers and Explanations
Algebra 2 Practice Tests

Answer Key

❋ Now, it is time to review your results to see where you went wrong and what areas you need to improve!

Algebra 2 Tests

Practice Test - 1						Practice Test - 2					
1	D	11	A	21	C	1	C	11	B	21	C
2	A	12	C	22	D	2	A	12	D	22	C
3	B	13	D	23	C	3	D	13	D	23	B
4	D	14	C	24	D	4	A	14	C	24	D
5	B	15	D	25	D	5	A	15	A	25	A
6	B	16	B	26	D	6	D	16	B	26	B
7	B	17	C	27	C	7	B	17	B	27	D
8	D	18	C	28	C	8	A	18	A	28	B
9	C	19	B	29	A	9	D	19	A	29	D
10	B	20	A	30	B	10	C	20	C	30	B

Algebra 2

Algebra 2

Practice Tests 1
Answers and Explanations

1) Answer: D.

Solve for x, $\frac{7x}{64} = \frac{x-3}{8}$

Multiply the second fraction by 8, $\frac{7x}{64} = \frac{8(x-3)}{8 \times 8}$

Tow denominators are equal. Therefore, the numerators must be equal.

$7x = 8x - 24 \rightarrow -x = -24 \rightarrow x = 24$

2) Answer: A.

Three years ago, Amy was four times as old as Mike. Mike is 7 years.

now. Therefore, 3 years ago Mike was 4 years.

three years ago, Amy was: $A = 4 \times 4 = 16$

Now Amy is 19 years old: $16 + 3 = 19$

3) Answer: B.

$y = 3ab + 4b^2$

Plug in the values of a and b in the equation: $a = 5$ and $b = 3$

$y = 3\,(5)\,(3) + 4\,(3)^2 = 45 + 4(4) = 45 + 36 = 81$

4) Answer: D.

$(g- f)(x) = g(x) - f(x) = (-3x^2 - 8 - x) - (4 + 5x)$

$-3x^2 - 8 - x - 4 - 5x = -3x^2 - 6x - 12$

5) Answer: B.

The diagonal of the square is 10. Let x be the side.

Use Pythagorean Theorem: $a^2 + b^2 = c^2$

$x^2 + x^2 = 10^2 \Rightarrow 2x^2 = 10^2 \Rightarrow 2x^2 = 100$

$\Rightarrow x^2 = 50 \Rightarrow x = \sqrt{50}$

The area of the square is: $\sqrt{50} \times \sqrt{50} = 50$

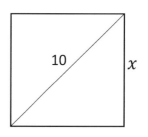

Algebra 2

6) Answer: B.

$(x-6)^3 = 8 \rightarrow x - 6 = 2 \rightarrow x = 8$

$\rightarrow (x-3)(x-2) = (8-3)(8-2) = (5)(6) = 30$

7) Answer: B.

$x = 45 + 118 = 163$

8) Answer: D.

By definition, the sine of any acute angle is equal to the cosine of its complement.

Since, angle A and B are complementary angles, therefore:

$\cos A = \sin B$

9) Answer: C.

$2x$ and z are colinear. $3y$ and $8x$ are colinear. Therefore,

$2x + z = 3y + 8x$, subtract x from both sides, then, $z = 3y + 6x$

10) Answer: B.

The question is this: 2.34 is what percent of 1.95?

Use percent formula: part $= \frac{percent}{100} \times$ whole

$2.34 = \frac{percent}{100} \times 1.95 \Rightarrow 2.34 = \frac{percent \times 1.95}{100} \Rightarrow 234 = percent \times 1.95$

$\Rightarrow percent = \frac{234}{1.95} = 120$

11) Answer: A.

Solving Systems of Equations by Elimination

Multiply the first equation by (−3), then add it to the second equation.

$\begin{array}{c} -3(x + 3y = 6) \\ 3x + 7y = 14 \end{array} \Rightarrow \begin{array}{c} -3x - 9y = -18 \\ 3x + 7y = 14 \end{array} \Rightarrow -2y = -4 \Rightarrow y = 2$

Plug in the value of y into one of the equations and solve for x.

$x + 3(2) = 6 \Rightarrow x + 6 = 6 \Rightarrow x = 6 - 6 \Rightarrow x = 0$

12) Answer: C.

$5x^4 + 6y^6 - 3x^4 + 7z^3 - y^4 + 3x^3 - 4y^6 + 5z^3 = 5x^4 - 3x^4 + 3x^3 + 6y^6 - 4y^6 - y^4 + 7z^3 + 5z^3 = 2x^4 + 3x^3 + 2y^6 - y^4 + 12z^3$

Algebra 2

13) Answer: D.

The relationship among all sides of special right triangle $30°, 60°, 90°$ is provided in this triangle:

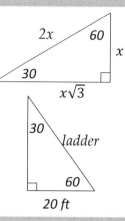

In this triangle, the opposite side of $30°$ angle is half of the hypotenuse. Draw the shape of this question.

The ladder is the hypotenuse.

Therefore, the ladder is 40 ft.

14) Answer: C.

Let L be the length of the rectangular and W be the with of the rectangular. Then, $L = 4W + 6$

The perimeter of the rectangle is 42 meters. Therefore:
$$2L + 2W = 42$$
$$L + W = 21$$

Replace the value of L from the first equation into the second equation and solve for W:
$$(4W + 6) + W = 21 \rightarrow 5W + 6 = 21 \rightarrow 5W = 15 \rightarrow W = 3$$

The width of the rectangle is 3 meters, and its length is:
$$L = 4W + 6 = 4(3) + 6 = 18$$

The area of the rectangle is: length × width = $18 \times 3 = 54$

15) Answer: D.

We know that: $i = \sqrt{-1} \Rightarrow i^2 = -1$
$$(-3 + 4i)(7 + 5i) = -21 - 15i + 28i + 20i^2 = -21 + 13i - 20 = 13i - 41$$

16) Answer: B.

$tan\theta = \frac{opposite}{adjacent}$

$tan\theta = \frac{3}{4} \Rightarrow$ we have the following right triangle. Then,

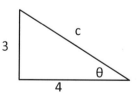

$c = \sqrt{3^2 + 4^2} = \sqrt{9 + 16} = \sqrt{25} = 5$

$sin\theta = \frac{opposite}{hypotenuse} = \frac{3}{5}$

WWW.MathNotion.Com

Algebra 2

17) Answer: C.

The amplitude in the graph of the equation $y = a\sin bx$ is a. (a and b are constant)

In the equation $y = \sin x$, the amplitude is 1 and the period of the graph is 2π.

The only option that has three times the amplitude of graph $y = \sin x$ is $y = 3 + 3\sin 4x$ for the one fourth period $\sin 4x = \sin 4\pi \Rightarrow 4x = 2\pi \Rightarrow x = \frac{\pi}{2}$

They both have the amplitude of 3 and period of $\frac{\pi}{2}$.

18) Answer: C.

Let the number be A. Then: $y = x\% \times A \to$ (Solve for A) $\to x = \frac{x}{100} \times A$

Multiply both sides by $\frac{100}{x}$: $y \times \frac{100}{x} = \frac{x}{100} \times \frac{100}{x} \times A \to A = \frac{100y}{x}$

19) Answer: B.

$|x - 7| \leq 3 \to -3 \leq x - 7 \leq 3 \to -3 + 7 \leq x - 7 + 7 \leq 3 + 7 \to 4 \leq x \leq 10$

20) Answer: A.

$\tangent \beta = \frac{1}{\cotangent \beta} = \frac{1}{\sqrt{3}} = \frac{\sqrt{3}}{3}$

21) Answer: C.

Plug in each pair of number in the equation:

A. $(4, -1)$: $3(4) - 4(-1) = 16$ Nope!

B. $(-2, 2)$: $3(-2) - 4(2) = -14$ Nope!

C. $(-1, -4)$: $3(-1) - 4(-4) = 13$ Bingo!

D. $(-1, -3)$: $3(-1) - 4(-3) = 9$ Nope!

22) Answer: D.

The slop of line A is: $m = \frac{y_2 - y_1}{x_2 - x_1} = \frac{7-6}{5-4} = 1$

Parallel lines have the same slope and only choice D ($y = x$) has slope of 1.

23) Answer: C.

When points are reflected over y-axis, the value of y in the coordinates doesn't change

and the sign of x changes. Therefore, the coordinates of point B is $(-5, 1)$.

Algebra 2

24) Answer: D.

If 10 balls are removed from the bag at random, there will be one ball in the bag. The probability of choosing a brown ball is 1 out of 15. Therefore, the probability of not choosing a brown ball is 10 out of 15 and the probability of having not a brown ball after removing 10 balls is the same.

25) Answer: D.

$0.7x = (0.2) \times 35 \to x = 10 \to (x+4)^2 = (14)^2 = 196$

26) Answer: D.

$g(x) = -3$,

then $f(g(x)) = f(-3) = (-3)^4 + 2(-3)^3 + 3(-3) = 81 - 54 - 9 = 18$

27) Answer: C.

$\begin{cases} 4x = 3x + y - 7 \\ 3x = 2y - 13 \end{cases} \to \begin{cases} x - y = -7 \\ 3x - 2y = -13 \end{cases}$

Multiply first equation by -3.

$\begin{cases} -3x + 3y = 21 \\ 3x - 2y = -13 \end{cases} \to$ add two equations.

$y = 21 - 13 \to y = 8 \to x = 1 \to x \times y = 8$

28) Answer: C.

To solve for $f(3g(p))$, first, find $3g(p)$

$g(x) = \log_3 x \to g(p) = \log_3 p \to 3g(p) = 3\log_3 p = \log_3 p^3$

Now, find $f(3g(p))$: $f(x) = 3^x \to f(\log_3 p^3) = 3^{\log_3 p^3}$

Logarithms and exponentials with the same base cancel each other. This is true because logarithms and exponentials are inverse operations. Then: $f(\log_3 p^3) = 3^{\log_3 p^3} = p^3$

29) Answer: A.

The relationship among all sides of right triangle $30°$, $60°$, $90°$ is provided in the following triangle:

Sine of $60°$ equals to: $\dfrac{opposite}{hypotenuse} = \dfrac{x\sqrt{3}}{2x} = \dfrac{\sqrt{3}}{2}$

Algebra 2

30) Answer: B.

$$x_1 = \frac{5y+\frac{r}{4r+7}}{\frac{10}{\frac{z}{4}}} = \frac{5y+\frac{r}{4r+7}}{\frac{4\times 10}{z}} = \frac{5y+\frac{r}{4r+7}}{4\times\frac{10}{z}} = \frac{1}{4}\times\frac{5y+\frac{r}{4r+7}}{\frac{10}{z}} = \frac{x}{4}$$

Algebra 2

Practice Tests 2

Answers and Explanations

1) Answer: C.

Set of number that are not composite between 1 and 20: A = {2, 3, 5, 7, 11, 13, 17, 19}

Probability = $\frac{number\ of\ desired\ outcomes}{number\ of\ total\ outcomes} = \frac{8}{20} = \frac{2}{5}$

2) Answer: A.

To simplify the fraction, multiply both numerator and denominator by i.

$\frac{10-2i}{-5i} \times \frac{i}{i} = \frac{10i-2i^2}{-5i^2}$

$i^2 = -1$, Then: $\frac{10i-2i^2}{-5i^2} = \frac{10i-2(-1)}{-5(-1)} = \frac{10i+2}{5} = \frac{10i}{5} + \frac{2}{5} = 2i + \frac{2}{5}$

3) Answer: D.

Solve for x. $\sqrt{9x} = \sqrt{y}$

Square both sides of the equation: $(\sqrt{9x})^2 = (\sqrt{y})^2$

$9x = y \rightarrow x = \frac{y}{9}$

4) Answer: A.

$(\frac{f}{g})(x) = \frac{f(x)}{g(x)} = \frac{7x-2}{4x^2-3x}$

5) Answer: A.

The equation of a line is: $y = mx + b$, where m is the slope and b is the y-intercept.

First find the slope: $m = \frac{y_2-y_1}{x_2-x_1} = \frac{6-(-4)}{4-2} = \frac{10}{2} = 5$

Then, we have: $y = 5x + b$

Choose one point and plug in the values of x and y in the equation to solve for b.

Let's choose the point $(2, -4)$

$y = 5x + b \rightarrow -4 = 5(2) + b \rightarrow -4 = 10 + b \rightarrow b = -14$

The equation of the line is: $y = 5x - 14$

Algebra 2

6) Answer: D.

The sum of all angles in a quadrilateral is 360 degrees.

Let x be the smallest angle in the quadrilateral. Then the angles are: $2x, 5x, 6x, 11x$

$2x + 5x + 6x + 11x = 360 \to 24x = 360 \to x = 15$

The angles in the quadrilateral are 30°, 75°, 90°, and 165°

7) Answer: B.

$3sin^2 a + 3cos^2 a = 3(sin^2 a + cos^2 a) = 3(1) = 3$, then:

$x + 3 = 9 \to x = 6$

8) Answer: A.

The sum of supplement angles is 180. Let x be that angle. Therefore, $x + 9x = 180$

$\Rightarrow 10x = 180$, divide both sides by 10: $x = 18$

9) Answer: D.

$cos\alpha = \frac{\sqrt{5}}{3} \Rightarrow$ Since $cos\alpha = \frac{adjacent}{hypotenuse}$, we have the following right triangle. Then,

$c = \sqrt{3^2 - (\sqrt{5})^2} = \sqrt{9 - 5} = \sqrt{4} = 2$

$sin\alpha = \frac{2}{3}$

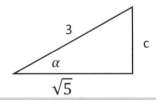

10) Answer: C.

Frist factor the function: $f(x) = 3x^3 + 30x^2 + 63x = 3x\,(x + 3)(x + 7)$

To find the zeros, $f(x)$ should be zero. $f(x) = 3x\,(x + 3)(x + 7) = 0$

Therefore, the zeros are: $x = 0$

$(x + 3) = 0 \Rightarrow x = -3\,;(x + 7) = 0 \Rightarrow x = -7$

11) Answer: B.

The equation of a circle in standard form is:

$(x - h)^2 + (y - k)^2 = r^2$, where r is the radius of the circle.

In this circle the radius is 2. $r^2 = 4 \to r = 2$

$(x + 3)^2 + (y - 5)^2 = 2^2$

Area of a circle: $A = \pi r^2 = \pi(2)^2 = 4\pi$

Algebra 2

12) Answer: D.

$7x^6y^3 + 3x^2y^7 - (4x^6y^3 - 8x^2y^7) = 7x^6y^3 - 4x^6y^3 + 3x^2y^7 + 8x^2y^7 = 3x^6y^3 + 11x^2y^7$

13) Answer: D.

Let x be the length of AB, then: $35 = \frac{x \times 7}{2} \rightarrow x = 10$

The length of AC $= \sqrt{10^2 + 24^2} = \sqrt{676} = 26$

The perimeter of $\triangle ABC = 10 + 24 + 26 = 60$

14) Answer: C.

$x_{1,2} = \frac{-b \pm \sqrt{b^2 - 4ac}}{2a}$

$ax^2 + bx + c = 0 \Rightarrow 8x^2 + 7x - 1 = 0$, then: a = 8, b = 7 and c = -1

$x = \frac{-7 + \sqrt{7^2 - 4 \times 8 \times (-1)}}{2 \times 8} = \frac{1}{8}$; $x = \frac{-7 - \sqrt{7^2 - 4 \times 8 \times (-1)}}{2 \times 8} = -1$

15) Answer: A.

Let x be the cost of one-kilogram orange, then: $5x + (2 \times 1.9) = 48.8$

$\rightarrow 5x + 3.8 = 48.8 \rightarrow 5x = 48.8 - 3.8 \rightarrow 5x = 45 \rightarrow x = \frac{45}{5} = \$9$

16) Answer: B.

Simplify the expression.

$\sqrt{\frac{5x^2}{7} + \frac{x^2}{49}} = \sqrt{\frac{35x^2}{49} + \frac{x^2}{49}} = \sqrt{\frac{36x^2}{49}} = \sqrt{\frac{36}{49}x^2} = \sqrt{\frac{36}{49}} \times \sqrt{x^2} = \frac{6}{7} \times x = \frac{6x}{7}$

17) Answer: B.

Let x be the number of adult tickets and y be the number of student tickets. Then:

$x + y = 16$

$13.50x + 4.50y = 108$

Use elimination method to solve this system of equation. Multiply the first equation by -4.5 and add it to the second equation.

$-4.5(x + y = 16) \Rightarrow -4.5x - 4.5y = -72$

$13.50x + 4.50y = 108 \Rightarrow 9x = 36 \rightarrow x = 4$

There are 4 adults' tickets and 12 student tickets.

Algebra 2

18) Answer: A.

Plug in the value of x in the equation and solve for y.

$7y = \frac{4x^2}{5} + 8 \to 7y = \frac{4(5)^2}{5} + 8 \to 7y = \frac{4(25)}{5} + 8 \to 7y = 20 + 8 = 28$

$\to 7y = 28 \to y = 4$

19) Answer: A.

$(x+6)(x+p) = x^2 + (6+p)x + 6p \to 6 + p = 8 \to p = 2$ and $r = 6p = 12$

20) Answer: C.

First, find the number.

Let x be the number. Write the equation and solve for x.

160% of a number is 80, then:

$1.6 \times x = 80 \Rightarrow x = 80 \div 1.6 = 50$

60% of 50 is: $0.6 \times 50 = 30$

21) Answer: C.

Let x be the smallest number. Then, these are the numbers:

$x, x+1, x+2, x+3$

average $= \frac{\text{sum of terms}}{\text{number of terms}} \Rightarrow 28 = \frac{x+(x+1)+(x+2)+(x+3)}{4} \Rightarrow 28 = \frac{4x+6}{4} \Rightarrow 112 = 4x + 6 \Rightarrow$

$106 = 4x \Rightarrow x = 26.5$

22) Answer: C.

Since the triangle ABC is reflected over the y-axis, then all values of y's of the points don't change and the sign of all x's change. (remember that when a point is reflected over the y-axis, the value of y does not change and when a point is reflected over the x-axis, the value of x does not change). Therefore:

$(7, -2)$ changes to $(-7, -2)$

$(-3, -5)$ changes to $(3, -5)$

$(4, 7)$ changes to $(-4, 7)$

23) Answer: B.

The equation of a line in slope intercept form is: $y = mx + b$

Solve for y.

Algebra 2

$9x - 3y = 18 \Rightarrow -3y = 18 - 9x \Rightarrow y = (18 - 9x) \div (-3) \Rightarrow$

$y = 3x - 6 \rightarrow$ The slope is 3.

The slope of the line perpendicular to this line is:

$m_1 \times m_2 = -1 \Rightarrow 3 \times m_2 = -1 \Rightarrow m_2 = -\frac{1}{3}$

24) Answer: D.

$f(g(x)) = 2 \times (\frac{1}{x})^4 + 7 = \frac{2}{x^4} + 7$

25) Answer: A.

$x - 5 \geq 9 \rightarrow x \geq 9 + 5 \rightarrow x \geq 14$

Or $x - 5 \leq -9 \rightarrow x \leq -9 + 5 \rightarrow x \leq -4$

Then, solution is: $x \geq 14 \cup x \leq -4$

26) Answer: B.

$\tan = \frac{opposite}{adjacent}$, and $\tan x = \frac{21}{28}$, therefore, the opposite side of the angle x is 21 and the adjacent side is 28. Let's draw the triangle.

Using Pythagorean theorem, we have:

$a^2 + b^2 = c^2 \rightarrow 21^2 + 28^2 = c^2 \rightarrow 441 + 784 = c^2 \rightarrow c = 35$

$\cos x = \frac{adjacent}{hypotenuse} = \frac{28}{35} = \frac{4}{5}$

27) Answer: D.

Based on triangle similarity theorem:

$\frac{a}{a+b} = \frac{c}{5} \rightarrow c = \frac{5a}{a+b} = \frac{5\sqrt{3}}{\sqrt{3}+4\sqrt{3}} = 1$

$\rightarrow$ area of shaded region is: $(\frac{c+5}{2})(b) = \frac{6}{2} \times 4\sqrt{3} = 12\sqrt{3}$

28) Answer: B.

Write the ratio of $7a$ to $6b$, $\frac{7a}{6b} = \frac{1}{18}$

Use cross multiplication and then simplify.

$7a \times 18 = 6b \times 1 \rightarrow 126a = 6b \rightarrow a = \frac{6b}{126} = \frac{b}{21}$

Now, find the ratio of a to b. $\frac{a}{b} = \frac{\frac{b}{21}}{b} \rightarrow \frac{b}{21} \div b = \frac{b}{21} \times \frac{1}{b} = \frac{b}{21b} = \frac{1}{21}$

Algebra 2

29) Answer: D.

First, find $2A$.

$$A = \begin{bmatrix} 2 & 2 \\ 4 & -2 \end{bmatrix} \Rightarrow 2A = 2 \times \begin{bmatrix} 2 & 2 \\ 4 & -2 \end{bmatrix} = \begin{bmatrix} 4 & 4 \\ 8 & -4 \end{bmatrix}$$

Now, solve for $2A + B$:

$$\begin{bmatrix} 4 & 4 \\ 8 & -4 \end{bmatrix} + \begin{bmatrix} -5 & 3 \\ -4 & 6 \end{bmatrix} = \begin{bmatrix} 4 + (-5) & 4 + 3 \\ 8 + (-4) & -4 + 6 \end{bmatrix} = \begin{bmatrix} -1 & 7 \\ 4 & 2 \end{bmatrix}$$

30) Answer: B.

The amplitude in the graph of the equation $y = a\cos bx$ is a. (a and b are constant)

In the equation $y - 4 = 7\cos 4x$, the amplitude is 7.

"End"

Made in the USA
Columbia, SC
12 October 2022